Due South

Due South

·

DISPATCHES

FROM

DOWN HOME

·

R. SCOTT BRUNNER

VILLARD

NEW YORK

All rights reserved under International and Pan-American
Copyright Conventions. Published in the United States by
Villard Books, a division of Random House, Inc., New York,
and simultaneously in Canada by Random House
of Canada Limited, Toronto.

VILLARD BOOKS and colophon are registered trademarks of Random House, Inc.

The essays in this book were originally broadcast, in slightly different form,
on Public Radio in Mississippi, and many were broadcast on National
Public Radio's *All Things Considered*.

Grateful acknowledgment is made to the following for permission to reprint
previously published material:

BRENTWOOD–BENSON MUSIC PUBLISHING, INC.: Excerpt from "Sing and Be Happy"
by Emory Peck. Copyright © 1940 by Stamps-Baxter Music (BMI)
(admin. by Brentwood-Benson Music Publishing, Inc.). All rights reserved.
Used by permission.

HENRY HOLT AND COMPANY, LLC: Excerpt from "Take Something Like a Star" from
The Poetry of Robert Frost, edited by Edward Connery Lathem. Copyright © 1949,
1969 by Henry Holt and Company, LLC. Copyright © 1977 by Lesley Frost
Ballentine. Reprinted by permission of Henry Holt and Company, LLC.

Library of Congress Cataloging-in-Publication Data

Brunner, R. Scott.
Due South: in praise of turnip greens, beauty queens, and sweet-
potato pie / R. Scott Brunner.
p.   cm.
ISBN: 0-375-50255-6
1. Southern States—Social life and customs.   2. Brunner, R.
Scott.   3. Southern States—Biography.   I. Title.
F216.2.B77   1999
975—dc21   98-49559

Random House website address: www.atrandom.com

Printed in the United States of America on acid-free paper

24689753

Book design by Jo Anne Metsch

For MaMa & PaPa,
and for my cousin, Mike

I knew that one's life, one's spanning of years and places, could never be of a piece, but rather were like scattered fragments of old glass.

—WILLIE MORRIS,
North Toward Home

APPRECIATION

———— ◆ ————

THE year was 1985, as I recall, and it was the first Post-it note I'd ever seen, a novelty my college roommate, Phil Ratliff, had picked up at the campus bookstore. But it was what he wrote on it that mattered at the time—a gentle reminder, taken from Proverbs, intended for me, the cocky student government leader who thought he knew it all. It read simply: "For lack of counsel, a nation falls, but many advisers make victory sure."

Thirteen years later I still have that note. And the words on it still matter. After all, the publication of a book is surely a kind of personal victory—one that for me wouldn't have occurred but for the patience and counsel and encouragement of many, *many* advisers.

There are my parents, of course, who, along with my grandparents, nurtured in me a Southerner's sense of place and tradition that shaped who I am, gave me stability and resilience. As my MaMa would say, "When you're firmly planted, you can bend in any wind." I treasure my folks—Mom, Pop, Tam, and MaMa and PaPa—and the lifetime of love and encouragement they've given me. This book is theirs as much as it is mine.

I cherish the persistent encouragement and gentle counsel

of my mentor and former professor, Sarah Palmer. This book exists in part because . . . well, she *demanded* it.

My aunts and uncles and in-laws and several friends were gracious enough to listen to the shamelessly self-promoting, homemade audiotape of my commentaries that I sent them for Christmas a couple of years ago. They flattered me by calling to say, "You should write a book." Thanks to them for their kind words.

I'm indebted to a cadre of friends and family who have counseled and encouraged me, especially my two ad hoc editors who regularly have read and critiqued my commentaries and on whose instincts I've depended: Catherine "What is your thesis?" Broadbooks and Katie "Are you sure you want to say that?" Bodiford. They continue to remind me to get to the point.

Others whose encouragement I've valued are Don and JoAnn Pate, Tammy and Mitchell Avery, Alan and Debra Robinson, Alan and Donna Pate, Kent and Vallarie Massey, Craig and Caryllee Cheatham, Norman McMillan, Chuck and Mary Ann Bearman, J. Danny Cooper, Cindi Bradley, Bobbye Moon Bullock Jackson, Tom and Gayle Reaves, Charles Dunn, and Marla Wynne.

I'm also indebted to my uncle Donald, who keeps me straight on family history and tradition; to the delivery man who stops at Uncle Connie's little grocery store in Parrish, Alabama, every now and then and tells about hearing me on the radio in Mississippi; and to the wonderful folks I work for (there are forty-three hundred of them; I'll not name them all), who are encouraging of my dual careers as association executive and commentator, especially Judy Glenn,

Cynthia Joachim, Charlotte Sadler, Larry Edwards, John M. Dean Jr., Jerry and Linda Brewer, David Stevens, and John Dinkins.

I also offer my heartfelt appreciation to the following people, who helped make this book possible:

- Producer Kevin Farrell at Public Radio in Mississippi and PRM Director William Fulton, who, in an apparently desperate search for local color, took a chance in March 1996 and began to air these commentaries and who now take occasional heat when some listeners don't like what I have to say (or how I say it);
- The loyal PRM listeners who have written, e-mailed, and called (sometimes at strange hours) to say nice things about my work or to try to sell me insurance, as when the twins were born; and the handful who haven't had nice things to say but whose criticisms I've tried to take to heart (even when they stung);
- Art Silverman, producer at National Public Radio's All Things Considered program, who heard my Labor Day piece and said, "We can use this," and who later came to meet me in Jackson hoping to find Southern cooking accommodating to his low-salt, nondairy diet (he didn't find it to be so, by the way);
- NPR executive producer Ellen Weiss, who airs my work, and NPR's Laura Lorson and Jeff Rogers, who see to it that I always have a piece on the shelf when one is needed;
- Jimmy Vines, my literary agent, as well as his brother, Matt, who lives in Jackson and convinced Jimmy to return my call; and

Appreciation

• The folks at Villard, especially editor Bruce Tracy, a marginal Southerner himself (West Virginia), whose great enthusiasm for this project is appreciated.

And finally, to my wife, Karen, my partner in birthing this literary child, I express my deepest love and appreciation. Thank you for supporting me in this project. Thank you for tolerating my airing the quirky details of our lives to Lord knows who-all. And thank you for allowing me to sequester myself in that little closet of an office at home, to write night after night when I should have been reading Pooh stories to Claire, Pate, and Jackson, or wrestling with them on the den floor, or gazing with you at the moon from the back porch swing after we'd gotten them to bed. May I not have missed too much.

This book—this personal victory—I share with all these who helped make it so. For their affection, advice, and encouragement, I'm immeasurably grateful.

And to you the reader, well . . . bless your heart.

R. Scott Brunner
Jackson, Mississippi
February 1999

Contents

——— ◆ ———

Contents

INTRODUCTION

———— ◆ ————

MY grandmother makes quilts, and her quilts are chronicles.

She's been making them—literally hundreds of them—since long before I was born, long before my mother was born, long before it was fashionable to hang quilts on the walls of fancy art galleries and sell them for a pretty penny as "heirlooms."

"Hit's just a quilt," MaMa would say as she'd wrap up another one as a wedding gift or send a couple more to the local children's home. "People needs quilts."

Yet there's been history—and art, too—sewn into every one she's ever made. It's a very personal history, admittedly, a private kind of art. Through MaMa's quilts, my family *remembers*.

She's not much into coordinating colors and fancy fabrics, mind you, so you're liable to find a swatch of red-checked gingham butted up against a square of blue-striped seersucker she had laying about. But that gingham likely used to be the kitchen curtains, and the seersucker is a scrap left over from an old homemade jumper my cousin Cortney wore when she was a toddler.

The whole family sends cloth scraps to MaMa, and so her

quilts contain pieces of our lives; they tell our story, remind us of where we've been (and often, what we wore). But they're not fancy. The colors and textures don't much match. Only a couple have ever been displayed on walls. Still, there's a distinct pattern in every one: the Wedding Ring, the Maple Leaf, the Trip Around the World.

The essays in this book are like that, too, I hope: simple, warm, and part of an overall pattern; a patchwork quilt of life in the South as I've seen it, as I've lived it. That's what stitches these dispatches together: life.

Nowadays, MaMa grouses some and threatens to give up her quilting once and for all; at eighty-one years old, she says she can't see to make those tiny, uniform, perfectly linear stitches like she used to. It concerns me, makes me a little sad. Then I'll go for a visit and there'll be the quilting frame set up again in the front bedroom where she always works because the light is good. A crisp new piece of cotton broadcloth, soon to be a quilt back, will be lying nearby.

"You still at it, Bess?" PaPa will ask, coming in the basement door and slipping off those old canvas shoes he wears to retrieve the mail or feed the chickens.

"People needs quilts," she murmurs.

And I need to remember.

Due South

Numbered Days

———— ◆ ————

IN the chill of January, she numbers her days.

She stands there at her back door—her gaze alternating between a view of the rear pasture through frosty storm windows on the back porch and one of those freebie wall calendars emblazoned with the Bank of Evergreen logo. On that calendar, with a felt-tip pen, steady of hand, she records the events of her life—those sublimely quotidian activities and images that mark her existence.

She's been doing this for as long as my wife, her granddaughter, can recall. There's always been that calendar hanging by the back door, its squares filled with things that, to her, are worth noting: what she sees through those windows, for example.

January 3	Rained, 2 deer in the pasture
January 18	Snow, 1 or 2 inches; feed birds
January 25	First day out since Saturday, saw 2 fox
February 17	Tulips break ground, windy, 60°
March 29	Snake on back step

In addition to her fastidious reports of peripheral flora and fauna and the day's weather, she also notes phone calls and visits and diversions; along with her own activities, the life events of anyone to whom she's close are duly reported.

February 20	Ed, Sharon & kids stopped by; didn't hear bell
March 27	Tax seminar; enjoyable
May 13	Salad for WMU social
June 21	Walked with Doris
December 9	Alan P called to say happy birthday

Perhaps her devotion to that calendar springs from a biblical admonition: "Teach us to number our days . . . that we may gain a heart of wisdom." Or maybe it's a by-product of coming up in the Great Depression—makes her treasure the simple blessings of each day and want to record them. After all, tomorrow may not be so generous.

Hence her thriftiness, which she wears like a good polyester double-knit pants suit. In her house she stockpiles dime-store finds, hides away useful sundry items in bureau drawers or in the dusty nether regions of closets seldom accessed, to await the day when she will need that set of porcelain demitasse cups or remember someone else who might. She even saves food. In the large upright Frigidaire freezer that sits on the back porch abide morsels of something from a 1994 church social, along with long-forgotten leftovers from some Reagan-era Thanksgiving dinner, patiently awaiting rediscovery and thaw for a midsummer night's supper. In her cleaning frenzies she finds things she forgot she even had, and her calendar is likely to note the rediscoveries.

April 5	Located picture misplaced at Christmas
May 8	Found lost items: old churn and oil brushes
June 19	Cleaned out old magazines and clothes

The only thing you won't find on her calendar is headline news, current events—well, not usually anyway. There are rare exceptions, always rendered tersely, incisively, with her own spin on exactly what is most important, most awful, most wondrous, about the event.

| *August 31* | Princess Diana dies in 4 A.M. Paris wreck |
| *November 19* | Frost this A.M.; 7 babies born (in 6 minutes) |

I imagine she pondered that last one long after the evening news was over—sat there contemplating the meaning of those seven new lives and their six-minute delivery, and the crazy, awful, wonderful world they'd been born into. I imagine her playing that story over and over in her head along with the other events of the day, like she does most days—scanning for God in life's details and, more often than not, finding Him.

Year after year the ritual is the same, for the very reason that each day, each person, each activity, to her is not the same. So pen in hand, she numbers her days, marveling at the wonder of her existence, and finding joy in the view from her window, the company of family and friends, and the occasional rediscovery of forgotten dime-store treasures.

The "Bless Your Heart" Rules

———— ◆ ————

IN the South, it's a well-known but unwritten rule that you can say anything you want to about another person as long as you . . . bless their heart.

I'm not certain of the exact origins, but I'd guess the earliest "bless your heart" was uttered in a semireligious context, probably by some parishioner over Sunday lunch to skewer a participant in the morning church service, as in "What that preacher lacks in substance he sure makes up for in volume, bless his heart" or "Bless her heart, if that organist hit one wrong note this morning she musta hit a hundred." And so the practice has evolved.

There are basically two levels of heart blessing.

A level one "bless your heart" is a sympathetic colloquialism—one of those definition-defying, uniquely Southern ones. We're not sure exactly what it means, but it sounds sympathetic and we're sincere when we say it. In fact, it's exactly what we say when . . . well, when there's nothing else to say. It's how we commiserate. We reserve "bless your heart"s for those whom we perceive to be aggrieved, powerless, treated unfairly, violated, infringed upon, or generally inconvenienced in some way.

Couldn't find a parking space? Bless your heart.

IRS send you an audit letter? Bless your heart.

Wife run off on you? Bless your heart.

You're the mother of three or more children under age five? Bless your heart—and heaven help you.

There's also the "bless your heart" reserved for babies, generally for fussy or homely-looking ones, always uttered in baby talk: "Bwess its widdle heart . . ."

That's a level one. Now, a level two "bless your heart" is something else entirely. In this more insidious—and interesting—form, it's the preferred way of pointing out another person's inadequacies, of mentioning what otherwise would be unmentionable in polite conversation. It's softer, more palatable, than a direct insult. Throw in a "bless your heart" uttered with the appropriate sympathetic tone, and a verbal kick in the pants is transformed into a reassuring pat on the arm.

"Bless your heart, Billie Sue, you put dark meat in your chicken salad," or "Arlene's hair may be blond, bless her heart, but her roots aren't," or "Poor thing got knocked up at the prom, bless 'er heart." Patronizing, yes—but it's always polite.

In the South, we've raised this second variety of heart blessing to an art form. Wielded correctly, it's a poison cherry dipped in the rich chocolate of genteel Southern "manners"; a condescending confection sprinkled with saccharin and sympathy; zinger masquerading as *bon mot*.

A level two "bless your heart" conveys at least a trace of real sympathy; it appears to be concerned while slyly drawing attention to someone else's flaws. It's the weapon of choice for taking a potshot at an adversary, because it can be done so darn nicely—sort of like complimenting a friend on her dress, then asking if she made it herself.

This kind of heart blessing is most effective in pointing out perceived inadequacies in someone else's intelligence or skill or personal tastes. For instance, "Bless her heart, Kathie Lee didn't know those clothes were made by nine-year-old Honduran children."

Or "When it comes to charisma, Al Gore's a wooden Indian, bless his heart."

It also may be appropriately aimed at beauty pageant contestants, as in "Our Miss Mississippi's a doll, but that Miss North Dakota, bless 'er heart . . ." In this context, it's a quaint way of saying "That girl should be embarrassed to be seen in that getup, but she's not. Can you believe it?"

That's not to say that "bless your heart" can be used with equanimity toward any- and everyone, at least when a Southern conservative is doing the heart blessing. Indeed, there are some folks for whom some Southerners harbor such scorn and contempt that they'd die before they offered them a sympathetic "bless their heart." With some folks, why beat around the bush, we figure; just insult 'em outright—they've earned it.

I'd wager the words "bless her heart" and Hillary Clinton have never been uttered in the same breath, at least not south of the Mason-Dixon line. Not even in Arkansas. Ditto Ted Kennedy, General William Tecumseh Sherman, and Boutros Boutros-Ghali.

Heck, even George Wallace and Richard Nixon were later rehabilitated with a "bless his heart" or two. But Yankee liberals are another matter.

The only other pointer I'd give to a heart blesser in training is this: you know you've mastered the art of "bless your heart" when you can do it, then leave the remainder of the comment unfinished, and the listener immediately perceives the inadequacy you're pointing out.

"That Dan Quayle, bless his heart . . ." The voice trails off.

Some things just go without saying. And probably should.

Turnip Greens at 33,000 Feet

◆

SUNDAY evening, wedged into a cramped window seat on a flight from Dallas to Seattle over a glutenous lump of something the airline called lasagna, I begin to dream of turnip greens. A mess of Mother's marvelous turnip greens, black-green, stringy, bittersweet, oozing juice, dribbling pepper sauce. And tender, savory, dried lima beans—salty, cooked with ham hock, sprinkled over with sliced onion. And corn bread. And a big ole glass of sweet iced tea.

I don't know why. Maybe it was the dreary, gray snow that I watched swirl and flutter outside the window at DFW Gate 13 before boarding the plane that made me long for home. Maybe it was the woozy result of inhaling the stale, twice-breathed cabin air that made me yearn for the aromas of the kitchen. Maybe it was the coagulated salad dressing and rubbery pasta dish, my in-flight meal, that made me sigh for countless plates I'd not cleaned before pushing back from Mom's table, for helpings I'd not finished.

Or maybe it was just frigid January that conjured up my recollection of Mother's answer to chilly weather and, at 33,000 feet, flung a craving on me: turnip greens and dried limas. Every other week or so on winter nights when I was a kid Mother cooked turnip greens and dried limas, stewed them until they could cut the fiercest chill a central Alabama January could muster. They were her prescription for thawing out, for warming my tender cheeks, red and stinging from the cold after an afternoon of romping outdoors after school. It was a weekly winter menu item at our house.

Funny I should yearn for it now. When I was a child, home-cooked meals were drudgery, unexciting, pale in comparison to the veal cutlet at the Bright Star Restaurant downtown or a pork platter from Bob Sykes Barbeque over on the Bessemer Super Highway. Turnip greens were tasty, but I dreamed of something more exotic . . . like the champagne meals they showed on the Eastern Airlines commercials on TV.

Maybe it's because I was reared on homegrown meats and vegetables. I was a first-grader before I ever tasted Del Monte anything—food from a tin can—and I wasn't impressed by it in the least. It was tasteless, textureless, flat. Some restaurants could dress it up pretty good, but it wasn't the same as home-cooked. Still, I preferred the *experience* of eating out, if not the taste, to staying home.

In my family we spent entire summers picking and putting up what we were to eat through the winter—literally everything from soup to nuts—two kinds of corn: sweet corn and field corn (frozen), Kentucky Wonder pole beans (home canned), butter peas and butter beans and squash (frozen), jams and jellies, vegetable soup, and of course, turnip greens (fresh until the first frost, carefully washed and frozen thereafter). There were fresh eggs, more than enough for the baking of pound cakes and biscuits and such; and fresh fryers in the summer, which often became fried chicken with mashed potato gravy; and mill-ground cornmeal. Octobers, when it was cool enough, PaPa and Uncle Donald would slaughter a hog, and then at Thanksgiving MaMa would hand out to each family its allotment of homemade sausage and souse meat and pork chops and ham.

And for years, PaPa's Yuletide gift to each of his children was a side of beef from his small herd. After the exchanging of presents, he would gather the family 'round the back of his pickup truck and parcel out the cuts of beef, frozen packages wrapped in white butcher paper from the Polar Locker in Bessemer, the cut marked in black Magic Marker. "We don't eat ribs much," Mother would announce, wheeling and dealing with her two brothers and two sisters, boxes and ice chests at the ready, and she'd trade Uncle Roger for extra soup bone or hamburger.

That homegrown bounty of vegetables and meats sustained us and, in many ways, made us into the kind of people we became: sons, daughters, grandchildren all. Not the food itself, but the sacrifice and self-reliance it represented. It also set our tastes and cravings, which would last us a lifetime.

I didn't know to respect or appreciate fresh vegetables and such back then. I was a child; what I appreciated was eating out—a no-more-than-occasional treat in my family. Yet with college—with eating mystery meat and tin-can-surprise *du jour* in the cafeteria—my appreciation blossomed. So did the cravings, when, as a bachelor for a while, I was forced to fend for myself in the kitchen.

I began to look forward to January, to driving north from my Montgomery, Alabama, apartment on a Friday evening and stepping into Mom's kitchen, and inhaling that awful, wonderful turnip-green smell and knowing I was home. I began to recognize that eating in, rather than out, was the real blessing.

These days, I travel frequently and often find myself despondent over a plate of congealed airline or hotel food. There's nothing exotic about it; I've yet to make one of those champagne flights.

So when I'm far from home on an icy winter night—on a Delta flight 33,000 feet over Wyoming, for instance—I crave home cooking. And what I wouldn't give for a perky flight attendant to stop her little cart by me, serve up a plate of steamy, fresh turnip greens, and ask if I'd care for a little pepper sauce.

Fox-trot

———— ◆ ————

AT the University of Montevallo, where I went to college, there are winter days when chilly winds scoot under the doors of old Bibb Graves Hall and race unbounded across the scarred pinewood gymnasium floor. . . .

Days when playful spurts of frigid air burst through cracks in the casings around the building's high, green safety-glass windows; when rusty old radiators mounted on the red brick walls above the entranceways hiss and sputter and click out a beat for the icy drafts to swirl and cavort to.

Chances are, there are days when the wind isn't alone in its breezy two-step across those pine boards, and that click coming from those old radiators has to compete with the giggle of sorority girls and the boisterous swagger of a bunch of college boys trying to veil their embarrassment at the fact that they're there in Bibb Graves to learn . . . to dance.

That's how I remember it anyway. Winter semester, 1984. Introduction to Ballroom Dance; J. Crew, instructor (the *J* stood for Jeanette—Miss Crew to us clumsy Neanderthals).

Miss Crew was a rather pale and proper spinster, sickly and slender and gray-headed, with tiny feet and a voice as clear and cultured as fine bone china. She taught several phys ed courses, but her passion was for the popular dance electives: square dance and ballroom, primarily. These, she made clear to us, were her life, and I imagined her clinging to a girlish fantasy in which Donald O'Connor or Gene Kelly or even Fred Astaire himself might one day stroll into Bibb Graves Hall, tell her her labors were not in vain, and whisk her, light-footed, away from all this.

In the meantime she was stuck with us, and she was determined to make the best of it.

We weren't exactly there by choice. Under Alabama law, college students were—and still are, I presume—required to take four hours of physical education in order to graduate. The offerings at Montevallo were plenteous: everything from softball and badminton to my personal favorite, a course called Golf for Business Majors. Each course was worth one credit hour, and they weren't especially difficult—well, except for bowling, which I barely passed.

Ballroom dance actually was one of the more popular choices. On chilly days we felt fortunate to be there in that drafty old hall rather than out on a frosty archery field somewhere.

A semester with Miss Crew began with the two-step, then graduated to fox-trot, then jitterbug, then waltz. I learned them all, save one. At midterm, I got bronchitis, missed a week and a half of class, and never learned to jitterbug. But boy, could I fox-trot.

I'd grab my favorite Phi Mu, Kathy McCarley, and we'd assume starting position. Miss Crew would drop the needle on the phonograph, and that drab gymnasium would suddenly be transformed into a Las Vegas dance floor, with Wayne Newton himself sliding down the chromatic pickup notes to "Red Roses for a Blue Lady." And . . . there we were, hoofing (and counting) across the floor.

I . . . want . . . some . . . red . . . slow . . . quick, quick, slow . . . slow . . . quick, quick . . .

Try as I might to go with the flow, I had to count under my breath. The smallest diversion—an intoxicating whiff of my partner's perfume, say—and I'd miss a beat, step slow when I should have stepped quick, and spoil the moment.

And what a moment it was. Fox-trotting made us feel charming and carefree and debonair. We doubtless were an odd sight: young couples in clunky parkas and scarves gliding effortlessly and elegantly around a dilapidated old building.

But never mind that. Never mind exams. Never mind cold. Never mind time. Never mind anything but Kathy and me and Wayne Newton's silky voice and that lovely, ephemeral moment.

Now, on days when the wind blows cool, I remember Montevallo and ballroom dance class, and I wonder who's fox-trotting in Bibb Graves today.

Sounds Like a Freight Train,
Tastes Like Chicken

———— ♦ ————

WE Southerners aren't all rednecks, but we do tend to play them on TV. Especially on the evening news. We could be Rhodes scholars, some of us, but you point a television camera our way and thrust a microphone to our lips and you'd think we'd just stepped out of the pea patch, the mud still on our boots. And pity the ones of us who *aren't* Rhodes scholars.

All it takes is for a twister to rip across north Alabama, and the next thing you know, CNN's running footage of some yokel in a Jeff Gordon T-shirt and Crimson Tide ball cap surrounded by the wreckage of his modest home, his Camaro Z28 T-boned by a fallen pine tree in the distance. He's telling a damp, earnest-looking reporter that whatever it was that came through there "sounded like a freight train."

Or watch the local news. Wait for the inevitable story about the latest food craze to hit town—alligator kabobs, ostrich burgers, steak tartare—it doesn't matter. I guarantee you there'll be at least one man or woman on the street who, when asked to sample the delicacy, will nibble a bit, chomp chomp chomp it, swirl it around in her mouth like Elly May

Clampett at a wine tasting, look pensive for a moment, then declare that "whatever it is tastes like chicken."

Trouble is, these aren't just any yokels; they're *our* yokels: our next-door neighbors, our in-laws, the guy who does our income taxes. We're even kin to some of 'em, and though they'd never be named to a team of expert scientists (bless their hearts), you know for a fact they're a good deal smarter than they look and sound there on *Headline News.*

And therein is the irony: in those media moments, when we seem to be at our unsophisticated, embarrassing worst, it just may be that we're at our endearing, ingenuous best.

See, I prefer to think—okay, to hallucinate, maybe—that we're smarter than we look, that our lack of pretension on camera is simply an accommodation to the medium itself. After all, television news subsists on simple images and sound bites, things common people can relate to and understand. I say it's entirely possible that we Southerners have come to understand this intrinsically, and so we give those reporters exactly what they want, exactly what they'll broadcast at five, six, and ten o'clock.

Take the tornado thing. Sure, we could wax philosophical, I suppose—quote Nietzsche or Goethe or Kierkegaard; mouth a pithy something about the frailty of life—but they wouldn't air it. "Save it for Barbara Walters," the producer would growl to his crestfallen reporter.

Maybe, realizing this, we Southerners opt for another approach: we choose to illuminate. Believing there's nothing to be gained by enumerating our losses, we pan the camera away from our personal tragedy and focus it on the beast itself, or at least on the pasture it rumbled across. With colorful simile and broad gesticulation, we seek to convey its mighty, wondrous power. "Don't worry about me," we say. "I'll be fine, I can rebuild—but this thing, this awesome, malevolent thing. . . . It was like a freight train. Do you hear me? It sounded like a freight train."

Not a passenger train or a steamboat whistle or a squadron of F-16s. A freight train. Perhaps, to the Southern way of thinking, the black, ear-splitting, churning power of a freight's locomotive is more raw, more muscular, more tornadolike than, say, the grace and the after-the-fact boom of the Blue Angels. A jet is too sleek, too refined. The simile wouldn't work: "It sounded like a jet." A tornado is not refined at all, and that, of course, is our point: we aim to illuminate the dark, destructive force that wreaked this havoc, not ruminate on the havoc itself. The freight train is itself an inadequate metaphor, but it's all we have.

Same principle applies to food—foreign, nouveau, or otherwise. Okay, maybe it *doesn't* taste exactly like chicken, but it's our way of stripping things down to the simplest of terms. Yeah, when the camera rolls, we could act like gourmands, discussing the nervy presentation and herbs whose names are darn near unpronounceable and how it's charmingly piquant or disappointingly flaccid on the palate, how the texture is reminiscent of this but not that and wouldn't it be lovely with tasso, et cetera, ad nauseam.

Trouble is, no one would understand a word of it. Much better to relate it to something common, something with which we Southern viewers are well acquainted, what with all the poultry farms dotting our landscape. And so it tastes like chicken. (It's purely a cultural thing, of course. I imagine that in Japan everything tastes like raw fish. Different strokes, I say.)

To a Southerner, tasting like chicken is the ultimate endorsement. "Why, looky there, Eva Nell," says the couch potato to his dear wife. "Womern on the TV says that new Dinty Moore potted possum stuff tastes like chicken. You gon' hafta pick us up sum'a that." Not only that, but a fellow could actually open a fast food joint in the South and serve nothing but armadillo on the half shell, and as long as he called the place Tastes Like Chicken, he'd have a hit on his hands.

So you see, it's entirely possible that we Southerners are not the philistines that the cultural elitists would have us be. It's entirely possible that we're just as media savvy as any Harvard law professor spouting his legal constructs and historical precedents. (Besides, how many Harvard lawyers do you know ever experienced a tornado anyway?)

It's also possible that I've been baking in the Mississippi sun a bit too long and it's affected my thinking. Although, as any good Southerner will tell you, it's not the heat that does it. It's the humidity.

Chap Stick

———— ◆ ————

IN the corner of a large, open room in the cardiac intensive care unit, my father lay flat on his back on a gurney, tubes and wires and hoses running from his mouth, nose, chest, and gut.

Pop's face was a pale gray-blue, unnatural, the color of rainwater as it runs off a gravel road. He looked absolutely lifeless, save for the steady whoosh and moan of a ventilator and the up-and-down of his chest as the machine "breathed" for him.

Nurses hovered near, everywhere, checking monitors, thumping gauges, reading charts, and taking pulse amid the whir and buzz of the life-sustaining equipment. I marveled at their fortitude and skill.

They'd shaved most of his body just prior to the surgery, Pop complaining all along. The orderly had joked with him about how much easier it would make wearing panty hose. Now his skin, normally tan and leathery, was dry and unnaturally cold to my touch.

I took one long look at him, then turned away. Despite my best efforts, a sob escaped my throat, and I pondered why at thirty years old I was having trouble reconciling this view of a small, vulnerable, terribly human-looking shape before me with that vibrant, bigger-than-life figure who'd been such a remarkable influence on my growing up.

His upper body was uncovered, and a huge bandage, secured by inch-wide strips of white tape, ran the length of his shaved chest. Just a few hours and four bypasses earlier, his heart had been troubled by blockages that only a week before he'd known nothing about. Surgeons had made an incision in his chest, sawed through his sternum, exposed the ailing fifty-two-year-old organ, and taking a vein from his right leg, somehow repaired it.

Now, supposedly, he was on his way to recovery. His appearance suggested otherwise.

And then our fifteen minutes were up.

Back in the relative warmth of the waiting area, with its institutional blue-and-gray-striped wallpaper, I considered the irony of the word "visitation"—at least in this context. The well-meaning nurse had called it a "visitation," but there was no sharing or exchange involved here. What we'd just done was "view the body." They'd told us to brace ourselves for the first "visit" after he'd come out of surgery, yet I was in no way prepared for what I'd just seen. But they said he was doing well.

Three hours later, when we were finally ushered back in, my mother and I were startled and relieved to find Pop awake, sort of. Still gray and cold, terribly groggy, but awake. A nurse explained again that he was doing remarkably well despite how he looked.

His eyes, half open, had a hard time focusing on us. A thick tube extending down his throat and into his lungs prevented him from speaking. His normal modesty was betrayed by a flimsy white hospital sheet that barely covered his hips. Better he wasn't coherent, I thought; he wouldn't like this one bit.

My mother kissed him on the forehead and smoothed his ruffled hair. Pop tried to raise his right hand to touch her cheek, but his arm was tethered to an IV line. Instead she took the hand and squeezed it.

She loosened her grip, and he began to wiggle his finger. It took us a moment to realize that, groggy as he was, he was writing. Slowly and clumsily, he spelled with his index finger on the bedsheet.

L . . . O . . . V . . . E . . . Y . . . O . . . U.

It was a major gesture from one so weakened. My mother brightened for an instant; the relief and emotion in her eyes were palpable.

The finger began again, spelling out another letter, but we were unable to discern it. "Try again, Pop," I said. He waved the hand back and forth slowly on the sheet, as if to erase his false start.

Then, slowly, he spelled S . . . A . . . M . . . U . . . E . . . L . . . ?

I smiled at this query, at his attention to the punctuation, and at the concern of a grandfather asking about the year-old grandson—my sister's son—he adored.

"He's fine, Pop," I said. "He's asking for you."

His eyes brightened for an instant, and then he blinked heavily.

I took his hand one more time, and for that instant felt utterly powerless to do anything to ease his obvious discomfort or to speed his recovery. His condition was in the hands of physicians and machines and God and the esoteric power of the body to heal itself.

I surveyed him—the pale face, the disheveled hair, the hose protruding from his throat—and my eyes came to rest at his lips—cracked, nearly bleeding, chapped lips thrust apart by an offensive (but essential) ventilator pipe plunged down his throat and into his lungs. Here were the worst chapped lips I'd ever seen. And here was opportunity.

I reached into my pocket, pulled out a small cylinder, and removed the top. I rubbed balm onto his lips, around the pipe, top and bottom, gently, carefully. He blinked again. And in his weary eyes I think I saw affection. Or relief. Something.

And I felt better, too.

I slipped the tube of stuff back into my pocket, squeezed Pop's hand one more time, and walked back to the waiting room, convinced as never before of the power of prayer and modern medicine and Chap Stick.

How to Rear a Southerner

———— ◆ ————

I am the obnoxiously proud father of a precious Mississippi-born six-month-old little girl named Claire. I am also the friend of a Yankee boy named Charlie, who grew up in Rochester, New York, and who last month started a new job down in New Orleans. These two facts are related.

Prior to accepting the New Orleans job, Charlie made a pilgrimage to visit us in Jackson, partly to see the natives in their natural habitat, I suppose, and also, as he put it, "To gain insight into our regional identity." At first I figured that was just his highfalutin way of saying "Why you folks talk so funny?"—a question I could just as easily have posed to him. Then he added a kicker. "I mean, you have a new daughter. What makes her Southern? How do you raise a Southerner?"

In my head, I heard my mother correcting his grammar—"Cattle are raised. People are reared." And I fought the urge to say it.

Instead I proceeded to pontificate broadly about Southerners' sense of place, about our being the only region of the country ever to suffer defeat in a war fought on its own territory, about the profound fundamentalist religious influences in our region—in short, everything I'd learned in my graduate course on Southern politics. Charlie seemed satisfied. We went to Lemuria Book Store, where he bought a collection of Eudora Welty photographs.

After he went home, I thought a lot about his question and my lame response to it. What *does* make a person Southern (I mean, besides the grace of God)? I've decided that being Southern is less about my sweeping poli-sci pedantics and much more about the minutiae of life in our little sacred corner of the world—specific, everyday things—what we say and do and eat, and how we think and dress and act.

So let me tell you my recipe for rearing a Southerner (with apologies to William Faulkner). Charlie, I hope you're listening.

Proper rearing of a Southerner begins with language. True Southerners have the innate ability to stretch any simple single-syllable word into a multisyllabic wonder. With a dollop of syrupy Southern inflection we can double or triple the length of practically any spoken word. Only in the South is *hey*—"hah-*ayy*-ee"—a three-syllable word.

We live by colloquialisms—words and expressions that we take for granted, but which at once charm and confound outsiders. Fixin' to. Y'all (or "you'uns," depending how far you are from the paved road). When it's about to rain, we say it's "comin' up a cloud." When a local feller graduates from medical school or seminary, we say "he made a doctor" or "he made a preacher." Our standard response to anything we don't hear correctly the first time is the quintessential "Do what?" Claire will develop an ear for such things.

Then there's the food we eat. A properly reared Southerner will have an inborn craving for anything homegrown or home-cooked. Sweet corn, butter peas, watermelon, fried apple pies, pole beans, grits, new potatoes, stewed okrey and tomatoes, blackberry jam, field peas with chowchow, corn bread, collard greens, sweet-potato French fries, souse meat (okay, maybe craving souse meat is a stretch). In addition, Southerners love fish fries and barbecue and corn bread with buttermilk poured on it (always eaten out of a large soup bowl) and casseroles made with Velveeta.

To a Southerner, Coke is a synonym for any soft drink—as in "You wanna Coke?" Soda is something you bake with. And we all thrive on sweetea (one word), the house wine of the South. These are all tastes my Claire will develop.

Then there are our customs and mores—the things we do, our rules of etiquette. Any true Southerner knows you don't wear white before Easter or after Labor Day, and we dress up for church. Our babies don't wear shoes to church, and we try not to eat foreign food on Sunday. We say "yes ma'am" and "no sir" and "thank you." A Southern bride can't get by without at least one deviled-egg plate. We own rocking chairs and keep them on the porch. We never honk the horn to pick up our dates. We try to know our next-door neighbor's aches and pains as well as we do our own. And we all understand that God, family, country, and the nearest SEC football team (in that order) are all sacred and worth fighting for. Claire is learning.

When you meet a true Southerner, the first question he'll ask you is, "Who's yore daddy?" The next one will be "Where do you go to church?" A real Southerner likes gospel music, has owned a Blackwood Brothers record at one time or another, and knows who Vestal Goodman is. And if every Southerner doesn't own a velvet Elvis painting, most of us can at least tell you where you can get one cheap.

Southerners respect tradition, know the value of a good story. We admire the written word because we still have among us some who are not too far removed from a time when our land was ravaged, our people destitute and hungry, and writing was the only thing there was to do. Perhaps that's also why we place such importance on knowing our lineage. Down here, we try to derive our identity not from our possessions, but from our roots—not from what we have, but from who we are. That's because our forebears learned a long time ago that everything else is expendable.

Claire will know most of this instinctively. As for Charlie . . . well, let's just say that like any true Southerner, I'm a believer in lost causes—especially where Yankees are concerned.

Poo-poo Builds Character

———— ◆ ————

IF it can be hurled, dribbled, dropped, spat, spewed, squirted, or otherwise projected from an infant's body, there's a good chance I've had it on my hands at one time or another during the past six months. For me, becoming a parent has been one lesson in maturity after another.

Let me say first of all that I'm delighted to live in the Sanitary Age, but I'm convinced that when it comes to babies, all this fuss over cleanliness is misplaced. Anything that can continue to grin and coo as it sits in pants full of high-level biohazardous waste probably doesn't care a lick whether its bottles are sterilized or its sleeper is washed in Dreft.

It was tough at first, me being the kind of guy who doesn't even like to get his hands dirty, much less have his necktie drooled upon. But my wife, Karen, says I'm getting better.

When we first brought our little bundle of joy home from the hospital, we were fortunate to have my mother-in-law stay with us for a week or so to help Karen and to train me. Now, "fortunate to have my mother-in-law stay with us" may sound like an oxymoron to some of you, but in this case, she was a godsend—or a real dupe, depending on how you look at it. Here's why.

See, it's a well-known fact that most of us daddies would rather go to the ballet than change a diaper, so we conveniently pretend that mothers don't mind it so much (a trick I learned from my father). Grandmothers, on the other hand, are like flies on dog poo. The way some of them jump at the chance to change a stinky diaper, you'd think there were coupons for Geritol or Maalox hidden in there somewhere.

Not only that, but for grandmothers, the discovery apparently is half the fun. All you have to do is suggest to Grandmama that baby may be soiled, and she'll have a finger poking around in that child's pants before you can say "Gah-rosss!" Then, with the dramatic flourish of a magician performing legerdemain, she'll withdraw the probing finger and—*tadah!*—"Someone's stinky. . . ."

But anyway, back to the point. That first week, my mother-in-law was generous in her offers to "let" me change our little stinker. "Are you sure you don't want to change her?" she'd inquire with a mischievous grin. "Oh, no, no. You go right ahead," I'd sputter, adding, "I'll have plenty of opportunities after you go home. You go ahead and enjoy." She fell for it every time.

But then she went home, and her daughter was not nearly so gracious. "I've changed the past seventeen diapers. It's your turn," my wife said resolutely.

"Ugh. Why do I have to do all the dirty work around here?" I'd mutter, and amble off to find a gas mask.

I've gotten better, though. I change three or four diapers a week now, and I don't even grimace. The goggles help.

Still, I'm not as bad as some guys. I've seen grown diesel mechanics—tough, burly men with grease under their fingernails—brought down by a glimpse and a whiff of the contents of a single baby diaper. They can cuss and yell for Dale Earnhardt with the best of 'em, but put 'em in front of a changing table and you'd think you'd asked 'em to wear a dress to church or something. I've risen above that, thank you.

I do get melancholy when I think about how our lives have changed since Claire came along. Our dinner conversation, once scintillating, has been reduced to sharing information about the color and texture and frequency of recent baby poo-poo. "Today was sorta green. Must be those peas" or "This is the fourth dirty today" or "Did you check her diaper before you put her down?"

Which brings me to my idea: diapers with indicators. Hear me out. Why can't someone come up with a diaper that actually tells you what's inside? Like, when she's clean, there'll be a nice pink happy face. She wets—it becomes a green frown. She dirties—up comes the Jolly Roger. No need to dig around and wonder, I say.

This could be especially helpful for posterity. Thousands of years from now, when archaeologists unearth an ancient diaper pail, they won't be fooled by those neat little white bundles wrapped tightly and secured with white tabs, because there on the package will be the skull and crossbones—the international symbol for "don't mess with this stuff." As it is now, a properly wrapped used diaper could be mistaken for an aromatic birthday gift by one who didn't know better.

Karen rolls her eyes when I mention this idea, but she does acknowledge how far I've come as a diaper-changing daddy. "You've matured," she says.

I agree. Apparently, poo-poo builds character.

Southern Provincial

———— ◆ ————

HERE in the South, we have a thing for nature—or at least something approximating nature.

This dawned on me one morning a few weeks ago when I eased my Cherokee out of the driveway and gave a nod to the ducks foraging among the azaleas in the yard next door. Down the hill, I grinned when I saw the little white bunny that sat sniffing my neighbor's petunias. I pulled out of our cul-de-sac and onto the adjoining street. At the next stop sign, I waved at the hobo swingin' on a lamppost on the porch of the corner house. I looked to see if the two black-and-white-spotted pigs, a sow and her young'un, were in their usual place, rootin' around in one of the flower beds on the side of the lot.

When I turned left onto the boulevard and breezed past the pond, I looked for the festive pink flamingo that occasionally perches there on a single, slender spindle of a leg at the water's edge. And just before I left the subdivision and wheeled onto the main road, I caught a glimpse of the deer, two of them, grazing tranquilly near the edge of a wooded lot, oblivious to time or temperature or traffic—all in all, a perfectly peaceful pastoral setting (well, except for the hobo).

And I have to admit, I was out on the main highway, halfway to work, before I was struck by the sheer goofiness of it: our apparent affection for lawn art.

I mean, what are the odds of finding a bunny, a coupla pigs, several ducks, an occasional flamingo, and a hobo swingin' on a lamppost, all semipermanently situated—frozen in time—within a mile of your suburban house? What is our fascination with Rudolph the Red-nosed Lawn Deer?

I'm guessing this is one of those idiosyncratic Southern cultural things—our penchant for prefabricated flora and fauna. Perhaps, in our century-long rush from the farm to suburbia, we've grown homesick for the genuine flora and fauna that once occupied our region. Now we only occasionally get a peek of it when an errant deer or fox or rabbit emerges from the wood and zigzags through one of our well-ordered, manicured little subdivisions or stands frozen in the glare of headlights along our state highways. So we compensate by propping a plaster pig or a spotted cow or even a wooden cutout of Grandma's backside out in the front yard, and we stab some tacky silk jungle flowers in the ground around it. (The jungle flowers are nonindigenous to the South, but that's obviously a minor point here.)

Momma 'n 'em may call it pretty. I call it provincial. Southern provincial.

By that, I mean a style just as pervasive (if not as attractive) as French provincial or Mediterranean or Scandinavian, but perhaps unknown to the likes of Martha Stewart or the buyers at Ethan Allen or Crate & Barrel. Southern provincial is more Cracker Barrel.

French provincial, of course, means curlicues, gilded edges, and buxom, bare-chested angels (that's a layman's definition, of course). Southern provincial, on the other hand, means lawn art and velvet Elvises.

A variety of stock lawn decorations are encompassed in this broad, culturally curious discipline. If you find it along Highway 61 in the Mississippi Delta or Highway 31 in south Alabama, or even in a subdivision off I-85 in South Carolina, chances are it's Southern provincial: planters made from old tires turned inside out and scalloped and whitewashed; bottle trees; cement casts of naked cherubs carrying birdbaths on their shoulders; and lifelike farm animals and wildlife made of materials that simply don't occur in nature.

Others? Well, that plaster cast of a shiftless hobo swingin' on a lamppost in my neighborhood, lollygagging on his way to the Big Rock Candy Mountain—he's Southern provincial. Ditto those "See Rock City" barns along I-59 between Birmingham and Chattanooga.

And certainly the once ubiquitous, now politically incorrect, hitching boy, also known as a lawn jockey, is Southern provincial. (A friend told me about a black family in Charlotte, North Carolina, who got hold of their own lawn jockey. They painted his features white and stuck him out in the front yard for all the world to see. I call this Reverse Southern provincial.)

Apparently, all of these in some way remind us of our roots, of the land as the good Lord intended it—fruitful and multiplicitous and vibrant with color and character and life—as long as they don't violate the subdivision's protective covenants.

Actually, it amazes me that, in some Southern subdivisions, you can't park your car on the street but you can sure as heck prop a plaster frog sittin' on a toilet and reading the news-paper in your front yard with immunity.

Whatever the allure, it all goes to prove that you can take the person out of the country, but you can't take the country out of the person.

Of course, it still doesn't explain that hobo swingin' on the lamppost.

Easy Street

———— ◆ ————

LIFE on Easy Street in the Bailey Avenue community of Jackson is not easy. There in midcity, Pleasant Avenue is anything but pleasant.

I know this now because I've been there, heard some of the stories, seen the poverty and filth and despair. Last week, from the sanitized safety of a rented passenger van, with a handful of my Leadership Jackson classmates, I toured midcity; and what I saw there was gut-wrenching.

The community I'm talking about is situated off Woodrow Wilson Boulevard, over past the sprawling, sparkling university medical center and the farmers' market, in an area of town where good, middle-class white boys like me seldom go in the daylight, much less after dark, unless they're looking for crack cocaine. It's a rough neighborhood where, for young black men, violence is the norm rather than the exception, and old people live out their days and their meager pensions practically under siege, forgotten by everyone but a few ill-funded social service agencies and their adult children and grandchildren, many of whom live with them. And the young women . . . well, if they don't work for wages, many of them have babies to care for.

In midcity, I see toddlers in diapers wander around patches of worn dirt that pass for front yards, scrounging for something to play with or perhaps something to love—something that might last for a while. I see their youngish mothers, infants on their hips, stare blankly through the ripped, rusting screen doors of rickety, dilapidated row houses that perch crookedly, dangerously, on crumbling foundations. Out back, rats the size of Chihuahuas scavenge for food along open drainage ditches. I see them. And on sagging front porches, I see old women of faith sit and mouth silent prayers for the good Lord to get them through another day, maybe help them with the light bill this time, too.

Up the way, I see young men playing basketball in the middle of a side street, on a court whose white boundary lines have been rendered crudely in leftover house paint. They grudgingly move aside for the van to pass.

Scattered among the occupied dwellings in this area are dozens of abandoned houses, their windows boarded up, graffiti spray-painted on many of them. "That's a crack house there," our guide says as we pass by one after another. "That one too. Probably most of them. And that convenience store right there—you can buy crack over the counter in there."

We come to a stop in front of a house on Pleasant Avenue. "This is Miz Daisy's house," the driver says.

Miz Daisy greets us at the door, bent over her aluminum walker. "How doin'? Come on in. Sit."

Miz Daisy must be in her late eighties. She's lived in that same Pleasant Avenue row house since the 1940s, she tells us; was married for fifty-one years to her late husband, who died in 1989.

"I seen a lotta changes in this neighborhood, oh yes. Lotta

changes," she says, and she doesn't elaborate. No need to, I suppose.

We ask if she's scared to live here in this neighborhood, scared of the gunshots that echo through the night, and of the drugs and thugs. She tells us she's captive in her house now, hasn't been out for months, but it's because of the bad arthritis that prohibits her from navigating her front steps. She depends on the kindness of her church and of her brother, who lives nearby, to help with groceries and medicine and one hot meal a day. "I stay in th' back uh thuh house here. Play th' piano some, when I can," she intimates. "I ain't scared."

Out of a plastic Jitney Jungle grocery bag slung from her walker, Miz Daisy pulls a cordless phone and a container of Mace. "This my gun," she says, deadpan. "All I need. Good Lord takin' care uh me. He will provide."

Faith sees Miz Daisy through. Others in midcity need something more immediate, more tangible, something more often than not out of reach. It is coming, but slowly. To a few in need, a few at a time. A handful of not-for-profit service agencies and civic organizations and churches are serving up hope in the form of tutoring programs for children, affordable housing assistance, credit counseling, job training, drug rehab programs, crisis assistance, and access to health care.

The current construction of a new addition to Galloway School, planted in the heart of midcity, will help: a shining beacon of hope—and parity—for inner-city kids. The new Jackson Medical Mall—a project whose very existence is an astounding accomplishment by a coalition of visionary black and white leaders—is bringing quality medical care and other services close to home for folks along Bailey Avenue.

But as the angels at Wells United Methodist Church—

those wonderful distillers of hope and help to the Bailey Avenue community—will tell you, abundantly more must be done, lest the future for midcity children remain as grim as the landscape there.

Sitting with my classmates in that rented van last week, the foundations of my well-ordered, antiseptic little world were shaken, and I was sickened and ashamed to stare full face into what my eyes have been conveniently avoiding for too long: gut-wrenching poverty. People hurting, right under my nose, and I've done nothing. Nothing at all.

I turned to my friend Chris, himself an African American, and asked, "Where do you start, how do you fix this? How do you give back to these people their self-esteem?"

There was a long silence as we stared out at the rotting row houses, sagging and gray and dead. Then softly Chris replied, "It doesn't really matter where you start. You just start. You have to start."

The Last Sevenbark
in Walker County

—————— ◆ ——————

IN the woods of Walker County, Alabama, where you can walk not too far in any direction and soon come upon the residue of overzealous strip-mining operations—scarred landscapes of scrub pine, blackberry briars, beggar's lice, and little else—the sevenbarks almost look out of place. Pity they aren't as plentiful as they once were. My grandfather says I'm mostly to blame.

That's because I've dug up dozens of them—hundreds, even—from the fertile Walker County soil and carted them off to flourish in such exotic Southern locales as Birmingham, Montgomery, Charlotte, and now, Jackson. Testimony, I suppose, to the assertion that the things'll grow just about anywhere, even in Yazoo clay.

PaPa says I'm sort of a modern-day cross between Johnny Appleseed and Lady Bird Johnson, going about beautifying the landscape, not with apple trees, but with sevenbarks. ('Course, the Appleseed metaphor leaves something to be desired, since I don't exactly bring 'em up from seed; I just relocate 'em.)

They're wild hydrangeas, actually. I'm sure the garden editor at *Southern Living* knows them by some highfalutin Latin name. But in my family, we've always called 'em sevenbarks because, well, they appear to have seven layers of bark— loose, thin sheaths like ancient papyrus, and almost as brittle. They grow naturally in the woods of the Deep South, often on the rim of a ravine or hollow.

I'm told they're philistine cousins to garden-variety hy- drangeas—the pink and blue ones that flourish on self-re- specting Southern lawns. Yet there's something different, alluring, natural, about sevenbarks, something at once refined yet untamed.

They're lovely. Unpretentious. Engaging. Too delicate, too lovely for a country wood, and yet not. The blooms are huge and long, sometimes a foot or more, full of nickel-size smaller flowers that bloom pea-green in midspring, then turn white in June, then yellowish in August or September or so. Come fall, they turn brown, and finally they're blown away in the winter wind.

They thrive in Walker County. Other places, too, I sup- pose, but especially there. Must be the coal in the ground— or what's left of it. And if there are fewer sevenbarks here than there used to be, it's because of folks like me. No crime in broadening their horizons, I say.

Each February I mention to PaPa in passing that I'd sure like to have a couple of sevenbarks to plant in the yard—you know, now that we're in a new house and all—and would he save a couple for me if he comes across any? As often as my wife and I have moved in recent years, this approach remains fresh. And coming across sevenbarks in Walker County is pretty simple. They're almost as abundant as cowpiles. Smell better, too.

Anyway, PaPa will look up from cleaning his fingernails

with his pocketknife. "Scotty," he'll say (he's the only person I know who still calls me Scotty). "Scotty, I think I've got one more sevenbark growing over on the edge of the pasture—my last one. You've cleaned me out. We might as well go get it and be done." And so off we'll trek, spades in hand, to uproot what may be the last sevenbark in Walker County.

In the ten years or so since I've been transplanting, PaPa says I've just about depleted his stock. He likes to tease me that sooner or later the Department of the Interior will come snooping around when they get wind of the decline in sevenbark population in his neck of the woods. Never mind that there are still parts of PaPa's wooded fifty acres that I've not plundered.

Truth is, we've raided woods; old, abandoned homesites; roadsides; cemeteries . . . well, I've never actually stolen a sevenbark from a cemetery, but I did snatch a little yellowbell bush from the edge of a field near my aunt Nell's grave a few years ago. The little thing now resides in Montgomery (the yellowbell bush, not my aunt Nell).

But despite PaPa's teasing, there's plenty of sevenbarks left around, as alluring as sirens in the hills and hollows of north central Alabama.

And you don't need to be a horticulturist or botanist with a degree from Auburn or Mississippi State to appreciate them. Graceful yet earthy, their apparent dignity belies their true pedigree as untamed things. They're like elegant old Southern ladies draped, on cool spring mornings, in intricately crocheted shawls of winter white; dignified ladies, some straight, some stooped and bowed, all clustered 'round a pine stump as if for a cup of tea or a game of bridge. You know their roots are in the land, but their bearing suggests something more ethereal.

In this part of the world, they're diamonds in the rough. On a summer's evening, under Southern pines, with their dappled, petaled frocks rustling in a soft breeze and reflecting moonlight, their leaves waving carelessly at no one in particular, there's nothing prettier than PaPa's sevenbarks.

Sure, a rose is a rose is a rose, but sevenbarks remind me of simple things, of PaPa and of home.

Mother's Greasy Bible

◆

MY mother has kept the same greasy old Bible on the night table beside her bed for as long as I can remember, and I've never seen it gather dust.

It's not fancy or pretty; it's certainly no heirloom. Dad bought it for her at the Master's Shop on Nineteenth Street in Bessemer at least twenty-five years ago. It doesn't have any marriages or births or deaths written in it. Its pages are dog-eared, its padded green covers scuffed and worn—just an old hardcover Living Bible, thick, with large, deliberate type inside. Strictly utilitarian.

In fact, to look at it now, the only remarkable thing about it is its sheen, a blend of Vaseline and triple lanolin lotion that's the result of years of use each evening just before bed, right after Mother moisturizes her hands and feet. It has its own essence: light, lotiony jasmine mixed with petroleum jelly.

It's taken two lifetimes (mine and my sister's) for her to anoint that Good Book, but the effect has been the same as if the prophet Samuel himself had emptied his horn of oil on its pages, dedicating it for the sacred purpose of rearing my sister and me.

When we were kids, mother never told us to read the Bible. Instead she showed us. She didn't boast about her nightly reading—didn't say anything about it, in fact. She just did it. And although I can't rightly recall when I first noticed her steadfastness at it, it left a lasting impression on me—not merely the religious and moral implications of reading a book she believed was holy and inspired, but her obvious commitment to it and the way it played out in her parenting. It told me that what she was doing meant something, was important.

Mom parented by the book—the Good Book. With that greasy old Bible, supplemented on occasion by the latest Erma Bombeck column clipped carefully from *The Birmingham News,* she was a compendium of rules to live by. "It's not fair!" I'd protest when, as a child, I would seek equity in my dealings with others and not get it. Mom would mention Job and murmur, "Life's not always fair, son." When I got the big head, as she called it, when I made a good grade or won a prize and was eager to brag about it, she'd turn to Proverbs for my lesson in humility. "Let another man praise thee, and not thine own mouth." Proverbs might as well have been a second language in our house, it was so often quoted.

Although she never ranted, she was not above some occasional well-intentioned nagging. "Don't slump, son; hold your shoulders up," "Tuck in that shirt before you come to this dinner table," and "Stop biting your nails—it makes you look insecure." She was not perfect herself, but she knew it, which made her work even harder at being a good wife and mother.

With Dad's complicity, she set high standards. Respect for adults. Manners. Curfews. Only one date a week, no more.

Pay your own car insurance, on time. If you want spending money, earn it, and many more. And while she never said much about dancing and mixed swimming (two offenses that were taboo in our particular church circle) smoking and drinking were absolutely forbidden—so much so that they might as well have been the eighth and ninth deadly sins as far as she was concerned.

When I learned to drive and began to date, Dad was fond of saying to me, "Remember who you are"—a reminder to behave myself and not do anything that would disgrace me or my family or compromise my values. Mother, on the other hand, didn't have to say anything. She simply expected it, and I knew it. Remembering that expectation kept me on the straight and narrow more times than I can count. My eyes may have wandered from the path frequently, but my feet seldom did. That's because even though I suspected the two of them could forgive me of practically anything, I was always darn reluctant to test that suspicion.

So I'd get home before eleven, stone sober, my virtue intact. I'd tiptoe stealthily down the hallway, and I'd see the glow of Mother's reading light. Having lubricated her appendages, she'd be sitting up in bed reading her text for the evening, while Dad, the night owl, watched *Mission: Impossible* or *Mannix* reruns or the *Glorious Ladies of Wrestling* on the TV at the other end of the house.

"You still up?" I'd whisper.

"Did you have a nice time?" Mom would ask softly.

"Yes, ma'am."

"Sleep well, son," she'd say.

Later, lying in my bed, in the eerie glow of the streetlamp through my window, I'd occasionally ruminate on Mother's bedtime ritual and the remarkable consistency of it. And eventually it began to dawn on me that what it all was about was renewal, reconditioning—first of body, with the flowery balm of store-bought lotion, and then of soul, with the sweet aroma of that old green Bible.

And knowing that, I began, in a small way, to understand my mother. I knew the source of her strength, the context for her decisions, the yardstick by which she measured the value and virtue not only of her actions and words but of mine and my sister's too. Hopefully, I learned from her.

Now, as an adult and a parent, I think often of that old green Bible and its oily sheen. And I'm reminded that some of life's sublimest lessons come not from eloquent homilies or fancy toys or grand gestures but from simple, quiet, consistent devotion to something you believe in.

The Fishing Trip

———— ◆ ————

TO my father's frustration, I never cared much for fishing.

Hard as I tried, I almost never shared the enjoyment he found in the ritual of it—rising quietly before sunrise, dressing warmly, packing tackle and life jackets and fishing rods into his pale green aluminum boat; the filling of thermoses and grabbing lunch packed by Mom in a brown bag from the Food Giant; the warming of the truck and heading off, first to Richard's Market for bait—crickets, usually—and on to the river; the sitting for hours, sipping coffee and eating— pardon the Alabama vernacular here—"Vy-*ee*-nna" sausages and crackers and waiting for something to happen.

I wasn't cut out for it. For one thing, as a youngster, I couldn't keep quiet, especially before sunrise. Getting dressed, I'd always manage to wake up the rest of the family with my clumsiness. For another, I fidgeted. I simply could not sit still in that boat, and my every movement clattered on its aluminum bottom, like Fibber McGee opening his closet. It's no wonder we never caught anything.

But fishing with PaPa was different. An experience. Sometimes an adventure, even. I loved my father, but he couldn't match a fishing trip with PaPa.

PaPa didn't mind so much the rattling about of a kid. He could sense impatience, the need for something to happen, and so he always managed to find a spot where the fish couldn't help but bite.

With me, PaPa knew how to set the stage for a "ride to the creek," as he called it. He'd start the afternoon before, telling me about a secret spot he'd found down on Lost Creek where a big ole bream or crappie or catfish would jump right onto the hook every time you threw it into the water.

"Why, the last time I was down there, my bobber didn't even get wet," he'd say with a sly grin. And he'd keep it up through the rest of the day, so that by eight in the evening, when we'd have "a little something cold before bed"—usually some ice cream or Jell-O, since both were his favorites—he'd have me so worked up that I'd settle for nothing less than a visit to his secret fishing spot that very next morning.

He'd wink at MaMa and say, "I don't know if I can show you my secret fishing spot."

"Please, PaPa!" I'd cry, and the next thing you know it would be just before sunrise. MaMa would be waking me, saying, "Get up, son! Wrap you up a biscuit. Your PaPa's hitchin' up the boat."

I'd scurry to get dressed, making all the noise I cared to, since MaMa was always up at sunrise herself, and she didn't mind.

I'd jump into the truck with PaPa and off we'd go to the creek or sometimes to the river for a morning of serious fishing and, of course, good conversation (PaPa was lucky if he got a word in edgewise).

And that was it; that's how I remember it. Oddly enough, what I can't remember is many of those fishing trips in particular. I can't tell you the exact spot on the river or the time when we caught catfish versus the time we caught bream. Perhaps time and memory have distilled them into one sweet, sweet recollection. Or perhaps, wonderful as they were, they simply can't compete with . . . *that time on the Warrior River.*

That's what PaPa and I still call it to this day, and it's been at least twenty-five years. *That time on the Warrior River.*

It was a spring morning, I recall. Just PaPa and me—he was fly-fishing and I was jabbering. Nonstop.

We had a system: he would catch 'em; I would net 'em. He navigated us to a suitable spot, cut the motor, and readied his rod.

His first cast sailed out, the line whipping, and the fly licked the surface several yards away. *Bam!* We had a bass, good-sized. As PaPa got him near the boat, I netted him, and that was one. PaPa sculled us along and pretty soon came another—then another and another and another, until there were nine on our stringer.

"Well," he said, "you think we got enough for your MaMa to fry?"

I considered it. "Maybe we should catch a couple more just to be safe," I said.

"You reckon?" he said.

And so we caught a few more. All bass. I don't remember how many. And that was it.

To this day, I can't put my finger on just what it was that has made that morning so special, so sacred to me. The number of fish, their size, the reflection of the water, the depth of conversation? I don't know.

What I *do* recall—what I do know—is that glorious moment when PaPa was still young and I was even younger, and the sun was warm and the river was clear and the fish would always bite and life didn't get any better than this.

Somehow, fishing with anyone else just never measured up after that. Besides, MaMa's cold biscuits and cured ham were infinitely better than Dad's Vy-*ee*-nna sausages. They still are.

Index Cards

—— ♦ ——

THE workshop facilitator placed a pile of three-and-a-half-by-five-inch index cards in front of me and grinned.

"Everyone take four cards and pass the rest on around," he told us.

I watched the stack of cards make its way around the horseshoe of tables, shrinking by four each time it passed through the hands of a participant. A dozen or more prospective leaders, hand chosen, half awake, sat fidgeting in sweats and Nikes, holding the cards and wondering what would happen next in this Saturday morning leadership workshop.

"This is an exercise in balance, in holding on to your priorities and not losing sight of what's really important," said the facilitator. "Now, take your pen and write down the four things that are most important to you. One on each card."

Silence. We stared at the facilitator. A couple of us shifted uneasily in our seats, already uncomfortable with the possibility of revealing anything too personal to this group of new friends.

He continued reassuringly. "No one will know what you write down. Think broadly, but be specific. What are the people or things or concepts that are the most important in your life? Write 'em down there, one per card."

A few began to write.

I looked at my cards, thought a minute, then on the top card, in my swaybacked block letters, printed *Karen and Claire*—my wife and child. That was easy.

I glanced around the room at the other participants. Some were writing furiously; some stared at their cards or the table or the wall or out the window, lost in thought.

Next card. Think. Okay . . . *Roots,* I scratched. *My parents and grandparents, extended family, a sense of who I am.* I shuffled that one to the bottom of my pile and looked at the third card, blank.

Hmm. Religion? No, not religion. Spirituality? Eghhh. Faith? That's it. My faith. I jotted *Faith* across the third card.

Last one. I heard the facilitator say, "You have thirty more seconds."

Yikes. What? Integrity? Well, yeah, but not exactly. What about professional competence—being good at what I do. Was that too goofy?

Our leader called time. I scribbled *Competence* on the remaining card.

"Okay," the leader said. "Spread your four cards out in front of you and look at them. Now, of those four cards, I want you to take the one that is the least important to you of the four and toss it into the center of the room. Just toss it into the center of the horseshoe here."

There was a pause, some nervous chuckles. Then cards began to flutter onto the mauve carpet. I looked at my four, picked up a card, hesitated, then reluctantly let it fly. Ouch.

"Good," our leader said. "Now, of the three cards you have there, pick up the one that is the least important to you of the three, and toss it into the center here.

No one moved. For the longest instant, silence seemed to lie upon us like one of those leaden, protective X-ray vests, as we each realized where this was going. We reflected, weighing the cards before us. I exhaled heavily, picked up a card, sent it sailing out. My remorse was instantaneous; a knot began to coil in my stomach. How could I have thrown that one away? What was I thinking?

I stared at the floor littered with cards, and flushed angrily at one that had fallen faceup in front of my table. *Good weather for golf,* it read. Here I was dissecting my soul, grappling with the agony of physical separation from something treasured, and someone across the way wanted to be cute.

The woman next to me sniffled, and I looked up to see her eyes reddening. A bright translucent tear plunged down her cheek as she pondered this symbolic but very personal divestiture of what she held most dear.

"You have only two cards left," the facilitator said slowly. "Take the one that is less important to you . . . and throw it away."

I agonized over my two remaining cards—tangible representations of things precious, irreplaceable, sacred—and for a while, I couldn't move. No one did.

He whispered again, "Throw it away."

Painfully I took one by the corner. It slipped from my fingers and fell silently to the floor near my feet.

"The exercise is over," the facilitator said softly. "Let's take a ten-minute break."

After a moment, people began to stand and stretch and head for the coffeepot or out the door and down the hall. When they'd gone, I sat there for the longest time, numbed, just beginning to come to grips with my choices and grieving for what I'd thrown away.

Someone Like a Star

———— ✦ ————

TO most anyone who has ever sung for him, Ted Pritchett is a bright light—someone like a star, to paraphrase Robert Frost.

He doesn't look at all like a star. The first time I saw him, he stood before us, stoned-faced, stern-eyed, serious. His mouth was set in a concrete scowl; his dark eyes glared at us from between reptilian eyelids; his arms were folded over an ample gut. He waited as we silently took our seats—altos left, sopranos right, tenors and basses behind.

He stood in the bend of a massive black Steinway grand piano at the point where the magnificent instrument's straight lines gave way to graceful curves. So formidable was his presence that it looked to me as if the Steinway's polished black sides had simply yielded compliantly to the force of his personality and detoured around him.

Here I was, a sophomore, and a finance major at that, wilting in the intense light of this . . . this star, the university's legendary choral director. Somehow, inexplicably, I'd made the cut, and on this autumn afternoon I found myself the least of tenors in his elite, sixteen-person chamber choir. I was intimidated, terrified, unworthy.

He cleared his throat and spoke four words without expression. "I . . . have . . . a . . . mistress."

It took a moment for his revelation to sink in, for my delicate, fundamentalist sensibilities to leap into indignant overload, and I was shocked. Shocked! Here was the kind of man my Sunday-school teacher had warned me about: a braggadocious philanderer bent on putting all kinds of strange ideas into my head.

No one moved; no one blinked; no one breathed as he stepped forward and continued. "Oh, I know it may surprise you, a man like me . . . but this lady is my comfort, my energy, my life. I fear I could no more live without her than a man could live without water or air. She has stolen me, and I cannot escape her."

He paused and looked up—a pregnant, dramatic pause; melodramatic, in retrospect, and just right for the spell he was weaving. I was scandalized, but mesmerized. We all were. Then he continued, *sotto voce,* "My mistress . . . is Music."

In my head, I heard the screech of brakes and the ugly thud of my simple-minded gullibility slamming against the windshield. A collective sigh went up and was absorbed into the acoustic wall panels, and we all knew we'd been had, sort of. Turns out, he was serious.

For me, that was baptism into Pritchett, the first of hundreds of wonderfully twisted, deadpan moments and vitriolic tirades and sublime musical lessons I'd witness and learn at the hand of the Great One.

As a musician and an educator, Pritchett burned with intensity. In his devotion to his art he was—and continues to be—consistent, demanding, difficult. Any former student would acknowledge he was hard to dislike, but not impossible. I've seen many a soprano—and even a bass or two—reduced to tears by his booming, biting, baritone sarcasm. I've seen alto music majors switch to accounting after a dose of his wrath. And I know a certain tenor who practically wet his pants whenever Pritchett glared at him in a rehearsal. He'd stop us and growl, "That's very creative, Mr. Brunner. Unfortunately, it's not the way Mr. Hindemith wrote it."

But oh, how the man could teach! With an ounce of that intimidation, an abundance of imagery, and a lexicon of colorful Yiddish phrases (he wasn't even Jewish), he gave meaning and feeling and life to stark symbols and words on a page. He adored Brahms's "Lovesong Waltzes," wanted them performed perfectly. We'd struggle with the German: *"Wenn so lind dein auge mir . . ."* and he'd growl, "Come on, guys, lemme hear the schmaltz!"

Or he'd pound difficult rhythms into our heads by scatting them, à la Mel Tormé.

Or he'd drill us on diction and phrasing by making us whisper a passage over and over rapidly until it was to his liking. "She walks in beauty like the night of cloudless climes and starry skies; She walks in beauty like the night of cloudless climes and starry skies. . . ."

And then we'd sing. He'd bellow, "Creamy, sopranos. Make it creamy!" And when it was right, we'd know. His eyes would close, he'd raise his chin slightly, and there would creep across his face this glow, this expression of sheer delight that was almost otherworldly.

Not long ago, I returned to Montevallo to sing in a special chamber choir reunion concert, to sing again with Dr. Pritchett—a sort of postretirement affair in his honor. For our finale, we sang the piece none of his chamber choir members ever escaped if they sang with Pritchett for very long: Randall Thompson's setting of "Choose Something Like a Star."

> *Some mystery becomes the proud.*
> *But to be wholly taciturn in your reserve is not allowed.*
> *Say something to us we can learn by heart*
> *   and when alone, repeat.*
> *Say something! And it says, "I burn."*

It occurred to me there that Ted Pritchett is like that steadfast star Frost wrote about—something heavenly and ethereal. Bright and intense and grouchy and excellent, he too asks a little of us here; asks of us a certain height—a commitment to our art.

For thirty years, he's been the center of Montevallo's musical universe, the constant, radiant, inscrutable sun around which generations of perfectly pitched planets have whirled and hummed and glowed, all delighted to bask in his light and know his celestial mistress.

Southern Berlitz

———— ◆ ————

HAVE you ever been to one of those truck stops or barbecue joints that have the placemats with the map of the South all out of geographic proportion, larger (and more grammatically incorrect) than life, and with a legend underneath that's supposed to teach you "how to speak Southern"? I hate those things.

Instead of celebrating the rich oral tradition of the South, those dumb placemats stereotype it, dwelling on our drawls and our predilection for combining words—the way we say "raaht cheer" instead of "right here" and "y'all" instead of "you all"—and glossing over consonants (and sometimes entire syllables). Such silliness simply reinforces a view of Southerners as dim-witted bubbas who spell worse than they talk.

Rather than making fun of our accents, it seems to me that a much more educational pursuit would be to highlight some of our more common Southern expressions. It's those maddeningly useful homespun colloquialisms—and not our drawls, or even our spelling—that help define us and are, in no small way, the coins of our linguistic realm.

Think about it. The words and phrases that comprise

Southern conversation are as smooth and well worn as river rocks, as colorful as aggies, and as comfortable as the driver's seat in an old Ford pickup truck. They're evocative and flow effortlessly from practiced lips. They may not all be pretty, grammatically speaking, but they're uniquely ours.

To the unindoctrinated, however, Southern vernacular may be confusing. So for the nonindigenous among us—and as an alternative to those puerile placemats—I'd like to offer this short survey of Southern colloquialisms. Think of it as a Berlitz course for Yankees in need of an interpreter.

First, some verbs: action words, like "fixin' to"—a verb phrase actually), origin uncertain, used to affirm some imminent action. It means "just about to" as in "Boy, I'm fixin' to tan your hide." And so on.

Next is "Do what?"—a verb question, really; quintessential response to anything you didn't hear clearly the first time. Basically, it means the same as "Come again?" which is to say "Stop mumblin', boy, and repeat what you just said." Unless, of course, you hear "come again" from the cashier at the local fish house, in which case it means exactly what it says: Please come back and eat some more of this greasy catfish of ours.

Then there's "Where 'bouts?"—part of speech uncertain. "Where 'bouts" is a more melodic way of saying "Generally speaking, where is it located?"—as in " 'Scuse me, ma'am, but where 'bouts is the men's room?"

Now for a few nouns. "Hose pipe"—you know, a garden hose. "Go git me the hose pipe so I can water this bougainvillea."

Next, "tee-tee"—a sort of medical term, actually; what the nurse at the doctor's office tells you to do when she needs a specimen: "Go tee-tee in this little plastic cup, darlin', and tote it down to the lab."

And then there's "boo-coo," an exotic-sounding singular noun. A boo-coo is an inestimable measure or amount, and most certainly comes from the French word *beaucoup,* meaning "very much." It follows then that the superlative, "boo-coos and boo-coos," means "very, very much."

That's not to say that all our expressions are as easily understood or defined. Some of the better ones, frankly, don't make a lick of sense. In fact, you'd be hard pressed to find anyone who knows their origin. But because we're so accustomed to 'em and they roll off the tongue so effortlessly, we continue to sprinkle them into our everyday conversation. Who cares about etymology, long as the meaning is understood?

Take, for instance, the directive "crack the window." Now you and I know that means open the window a little bit and let some breeze in. But to the uninitiated, it sounds like you're encouraging property damage. And in the summer, we say "turn the air up" when what we really want is for someone to turn the thermostat down.

And down here, after we shell our fresh butter beans or peas, we "look" 'em, which is to say we look at them, scrutinize them, a handful at a time, and throw out the ones that have been gnawed on by little worms and are brown and spoiled. All that is preliminary, of course, to "puttin' 'em up," which is to say, canning them, which is itself a misnomer since canning in the South actually involves a glass Mason jar and a pressure cooker, and not a can. Sorta complicated, huh?

Finally, there are the "pejoratives"—colorful figures of speech that arose from situations long forgotten, but that are locked into our Southern dialect as mildly defamatory descriptions. For instance, "drunk as Cooter Brown." This one most certainly refers to an extreme degree of intoxication. But *who was* the much-maligned Mr. Brown? And why does his name endure as the apotheosis of public insobriety in the South?

Also "Ned 'n the first reader." This apparently refers to disheveled and unwashed little boys, 'cause it's what my grandmother always said when I'd come to the dinner table after a morning of playing in the storm cellar: "Son, go wash up. You look like Ned 'n the first reader." I have to admit, her meaning was lost on me, but it was preferable to being told I looked like "sump'n a horse dropped"—an expression I once heard a college buddy of mine from east Alabama, ever the diplomat, use in describing one of our hungover fraternity brothers.

And there you have it: a good primer in basic Southern. Not to suggest that it's an exhaustive list, but propriety and the early hour don't permit me to discuss the genesis of such other Southern expressions like "dog ugly," "breaking wind," and the like. This will just have to do for the time being.

Now if I can just figure out how to fit it all on one of those placemats.

Walking

———— ◆ ————

MY little girl, Claire, turned one the other day, and on the afternoon of her birthday, I stood in the doorway of her cheery little room and watched her napping. After twelve months, I still can't stop looking at her—and that's a good thing. If I were to blink, I might miss something significant.

In the past two weeks alone she learned "doggie" and "cow," and now she says "gotta go" when she wants to ride in the car. She's finally learned how to sit herself back down after pulling up to a standing position on the coffee table; and she's shown the first signs of understanding that Mommy will allow only so many Cheerios to hit the floor before Mommy takes them away.

Claire can almost walk now—almost—although she doesn't much care for it. She's more fleet of hand and knee than of foot at this point, and she whines a lot and tends to plop down on her fanny when we stand her upright.

But although the mechanics (and allure) of walking apparently elude her right now, she's nevertheless very bright (of course). As of this week, we can identify almost thirty words she knows and can say, and if she's not yet ready for freshman comp or German lessons, she can nevertheless hold her own in a confab with a child twice her age.

She'll walk eventually. Me too, I hope. I've fallen on my figurative fanny more than a few times in the past twelve months as I've tried to keep pace with her growth. Who'd have thought Daddy and baby would learn to walk together?

I expected there to be some rules, a manual or something. "Do these things and have a well-adjusted child, guaranteed"—something like that. Instead I'm realizing that there's more to fathering than can be gleaned from last month's issue of *Parenting,* or even from a talk with my dad. It's sorta like, well, learning to walk. External support will only get you so far, then it's up to you.

Mothers, I suspect, have known this for centuries, but then, they come equipped with maternal instinct. We daddies generally aren't so sophisticated—at least not at first. In the delivery room, a nurse thrusts a squalling bundle into our arms, and there we are, fathering for the video camera. Inside, though, we're as disoriented as the newborn, just as pitiful but not nearly as cute. At that moment, the only thing we can do instinctively as we try not to bobble the bundle is worry about how we're gonna pay for braces and college tuition.

We spend the next twelve months or so flailing about—ruing the reproductive process that created our disequilibrium, wondering why Mommy is so grumpy, longing to do something spontaneous, like catch a movie. In the wee hours of the morning, to the tune of an infant's wailing, we sort through our feelings of inadequacy, trying groggily to get a handle on exactly what being a Daddy is supposed to mean.

And then, suddenly we're crawling—I mean, the baby's crawling, and Daddy's doing okay, too. Curiously, having gotten past the initial trauma brought on by that dose of awesome responsibility in the delivery room, our on-the-job training has given rise to a visceral understanding of our role as fathers. Maybe a paternal instinct, albeit a late-blooming one, exists after all. If so, it's not from the gut, not the kind of preservation instinct that pushes into our male psyches with the confidence and swagger of a vacuum cleaner salesman throwing dirt on the rug. Not quite. Instead, a daddy's instinct is riddled with nuance: tender, yet firm; sharp, but loving; as delicately balanced as a Calder sculpture, just not quite as graceful.

Listening to my emerging instinct requires every bit as much poise and balance and circumspection as Claire's reluctant first steps do. It means weighing my words and actions, knowing what to say and how to say it, when to hold and when to hush, and how to fix things when I mess it all up. It often means forgoing the evening news in favor of tumbling on the floor. It means less me, more us.

Most of all, it means walking the talk. Neophyte that I am, I'm just beginning to grapple with the unmitigated influence I apparently have as a father, just beginning to fathom the power of my example. The other morning, as usual, I stood in front of the mirror in the bathroom, readying myself for work, drying my hair. I looked down at my feet and there was Claire, on her knees, doing her hair, mimicking my every movement with imaginary hairbrush and dryer. "Daddy," she said, and patted the top of her head.

Sure, it was cute, but it also was epiphany. There, staring blankly into the bathroom mirror, I saw the real challenge of fatherhood: to be, in my daughter's eyes, exactly what I profess to be; to practice what I preach.

And there's the rub. Precepts I can ladle out. It's the role-modeling that'll keep me on my toes. Just thinking of all the bad habits I need to change—my wife says I should start with my driving—gives me a headache. Oh, to be a babe with someone to mimic. I'm sure I'll fall on my fanny plenty more times. And I'll have to get right back up and try again. After all, that's what I'm teaching my child.

Claire can almost walk now—almost—and although she doesn't much care for it, some days it feels like she's progressing faster than I am, and I wonder if I'm going to be ready for that next developmental stunt she's sure to pull. Today it's teaching her not to eat the houseplants, not to rip pages out of Mommy's *Southern Living* magazine, that "no" means "no." Tomorrow it's teaching her to share, to say "yes sir" and "no ma'am"; to assuage her fears and to respond appropriately to myriad impossible questions she's bound to ask. Then comes getting her ears pierced and dating, and I don't even want to think about that right now.

Gotta learn to walk first, one step at a time, both of us.

Come Out, Eudora
(Wherever You Are)

———— ◆ ————

REMEMBER that scene in *To Kill a Mockingbird,* the one where Jem and Scout throw rocks at the house next door, to try and get its reclusive occupant, Boo Radley, to come out? Reminds me of my friends Larry and Emmy. Awhile back, they moved into a house in the Belhaven section of Jackson, and I've never seen two folks so eager to meet their next-door neighbor.

'Course, I've never known anyone who lived right next door to Eudora Welty, either.

Her house is on Pinehurst Street in Belhaven, just up the street from the Jitney No. 14 made famous in Miz Welty's acclaimed reminiscences. After Larry and Emmy moved in next door, meeting the reclusive celebrity apparently became something of an obsession for them.

Not long ago, my wife and I had dinner with them and heard their story.

It appears that Emmy did everything but bake cookies and send them over. Hey, you're the newcomers, we reminded her. If anything, Miz Welty should have sent you cookies.

Larry said he was hoping for an autographed copy of *One Writer's Beginnings.* "I mean, years from now, how many people will be able to say they once met Eudora Welty?" he asked us. "It's like meeting Faulkner or Fitzgerald."

Yeah, I countered, but by the same token, how many folks can say they once *lived next door* to Eudora Welty? Isn't that enough?

They shook their heads in unison.

Emmy chimed in. "You know, the couple who owned the house right before us actually got a phone call from her right after they moved in. They told us about it at the real estate closing. This house, as you know, is a two-story, just like Miz Welty's, and the master bedroom is upstairs, apparently directly across from what was Miz Welty's bedroom at the time."

Larry picked it up from there. "The new neighbors had been in the house just a few days, still in the process of getting settled, when one afternoon their phone rings. 'Hello, this is Eudora Welty, your next-door neighbor. You people need to either put some curtains on your bedroom window or start wearing clothes.' "

It's an amusing story, whether it's true or not, and we laugh. But I know secretly we're all weighing whether, if given proximity and opportunity, we'd go so far as to gallivant naked in front of the window if it meant we might get to talk with the grande dame of Southern letters.

Emmy said she actually considered an ambush. She wanted to dash next door with her year-old son, Sumner, ring the bell, and when by some miracle the Pulitzer Prize winner herself answered the door, Emmy would thrust Sumner into Miz Welty's arms and snap a quick photo.

My mind raced, and for an instant I could envision Miz Welty with a pained, shocked look on her face as Sumner screamed and squirmed in her frail arms. A regular Kodak moment.

"Why not?" Emmy says wryly. "That picture would have been one of a kind. I could have apologized later, after I got to know her."

Yeah, I thought to myself, provided the surprise didn't give the poor woman a palpitation. I could see it on the front page of the Jackson newspaper—heck, *The New York Times,* for that matter—"Pulitzer Prize winner accosted by ambitious neighbor; swoons on front porch." CNN would come to town and interview Larry's and Emmy's few remaining friends: was the assailant always crazy or was it temporary insanity brought about by close proximity to a Pulitzer Prize winner? And Willie Morris would write a moving piece in *Harper's* bemoaning the heartless attack on Mississippi's literary matriarch and holding the incident up as evidence of the decay of traditional Southern manners. Then they'd convict Emmy and cart her off to the funny farm, where, as part of her punishment, there'd be nothing to read but Sidney Sheldon and Danielle Steele.

Larry, on the other hand, chose a less theatrical, more subtle approach. He went and knocked on Miz Welty's front door. He tried it twice and was stopped short both times by Miz Welty's nurse, who politely reminded him that the Legion of Honor recipient was feeling poorly and could not see him.

But persistence eventually paid off, aided by Larry and Emmy's yapping dog. One Sunday, after church, they met the great writer as she was helped to her car by a friend, and they chatted briefly. "I like your little dog," she said. "I can see him in your backyard from my bedroom window."

Thankfully, that was enough to put Emmy's schemes to rest.

At least she didn't resort to throwing rocks at Miz Welty's house, like Jem and Scout did to Boo Radley in *To Kill a Mockingbird*. I'm just glad she didn't think of it.

Arthur's

———— ◆ ————

NOT long ago, at a barbecue joint in Collins, Mississippi, I found the South.

What I was looking for was a chopped-pork sandwich and a glass of iced tea, and I found those, too—at Arthur's, a roadside hole-in-the-wall on Highway 49 North. The rest was pure serendipity—finding the South, I mean. I didn't even realize it was missing. All I know is that if the South has been AWOL, it only seems natural that I'd find it at a place like Arthur's—a place where the drawls are as thick as the barbecue sauce and as sweet and refreshing as a quart jar of forty-weight iced tea.

I can only guess at what compelled me to wheel into Arthur's gravel parking lot that afternoon. I'd been in Biloxi that morning for a business meeting at one of those casino hotels that float like garish prostitutes in neon feather boas along Mississippi Beach. Visits there always leave me melancholy, torn by my grudging appreciation for the economic windfall that riverboat gaming has brought to the state and my sense that we're losing something irreplaceable (some of our identity maybe?) in the transaction.

So by the time I pointed my car back toward Jackson—late

morning—I felt like Scarlett O'Hara surveying the ruins of Atlanta. Plus I'd skipped breakfast, and I was hungry. With a smidgen of righteous indignation, I reminded myself that Real Southerners Don't Eat Fast Food (not regularly, anyway), and I whizzed on past McDonald's and Taco Bell without so much as a blink, in search of more indigenous fare.

North of Hattiesburg, approaching famished, I spotted the billboard: ARTHUR'S BARBECUE 2 MILES. Something clicked in my head, and the next thing I knew I was pulling open Arthur's heavy glass front door, cool, climate-controlled air was washing over me, and I was nodding politely at a pretty brunette who asked me if she could take my order.

I scanned the menu, which consisted of six, maybe seven, items tops. Not a Value Meal or Super-Size price in sight. "Two pork sandwiches, sweetea, to go."

She scribbled on her pad, turned to hand it through the window to the kitchen, and returned smiling to ring up my order. "Be just a minute 'r two," she said. I paid her, then took a seat to wait.

It was my first chance to really get a look at the place. It was . . . comfortable. Simple. Unpretentious. Exactly what you'd expect it to be, in fact. On the wall above my head, a framed poster depicted two mature-looking three-year-olds in overalls standing on a tractor path. One was saying to the other, "Been farming long?" Across the way, a bulletin board was papered with handbills advertising revivals and lost dogs and income tax preparers and piano lessons.

About that time, a couple of fragile-looking elderly ladies in polyester shirtwaist dresses came in and tottered over to a table for two. I knew they were Southern ladies by the violet tint of their coiffed hair, by the way one clung to the other's arm in a display of sisterly support, and by the dainty way they lugged their black patent leather purses on their forearms. They looked as though they hadn't been out in years, had suddenly gotten a hankering for some ribs, and like a geriatric Thelma and Louise, had decided to turn it into a spree.

"Hey there, ladies, have a seat. I'll be with you in a sec," said the brunette waitress as she made the rounds with the iced tea pitcher.

The old girls perused the menu and I watched them while I waited for my order. The one with the stronger bifocals was helping the other interpret the fine print. "Pork plate, you say?" asked the more myopic of the two loudly.

"Thass right," said the other, patting her friend's arm.

In the center of the room, five men—farmers, I guessed—were seated around a table, sipping iced tea. They all looked to be my father's age (fiftyish), with tanned, leathery skin and serious eyes, and all wore Levi's and brogans and ball caps that sat high over their thinning pates and advertised a brand of auto parts or herbicide. They talked about soybean yields and the weather as they waited, and occasionally one would say something funny and they'd all guffaw. Then, shortly, when their order came, I watched as they each doffed their caps, bowed their heads, and one of them, in a red plaid shirt, said the blessing.

Two thirty-something guys, one black, one white, sat near the cash register, and one was trying to convince the other, over a plate of ribs, that leasing a pickup was to be preferred over purchasing one outright, "especially if you aim to trade every three years or so anyway, Kenny," he said. "Don't make sense not to," he added, licking his fingers.

The brunette called to me cheerily, "Mister, here's your order."

Only upon reflection, back in my car, miles up the highway, did it dawn on me that what I'd witnessed was the real South, stripped down, simple, sincere.

These days, folks eulogize the South and blame its demise on everything from Wal-Mart and mass marketing to interstate highways and the Internet. Maybe they're right. But the South they long for is abstract—not a region, not lines on a map, not stereotypes of belles and bubbas and poverty and racism, but a sense of place. It's an understanding of who we are; it's a recollection of the past and a genuine hope for the future; and it's a set of more widely held attitudes of kindness and civility and appreciation.

I'm guessing that those folks—the ones who say the South is lost—are just looking for it in the wrong places. It may not be at Harrah's casino or under the Golden Arches or anywhere near an interstate highway, with those cookie-cutter shopping centers and chain stores. Instead, the South is right where it's always been—off the beaten path, among the folks in places like Arthur's Barbecue in Collins, Mississippi, where the smiles are genuine and talk of the weather is scintillating; where little old ladies take lunch and help each other along; where farmers trade fishing stories and bow their heads to give thanks; and where a Southern boy can get a delicious pork sandwich and an iced tea at a fair price.

I found the South at Arthur's, and it was on the house.

Shirley Goodness
and the Cross-eyed Bear

———— ◆ ————

WHEN I was a child, I understood as a child—which made for some pretty interesting interpretations of the songs we sang at church.

I grew up in the South in the Church of Christ, fellowships best known for their wonderful a cappella singing tradition. In country churches, however, where I spent a lot of that growing-up time, "wonderful" wasn't always a word you could use to describe the music.

There, in simple, whitewashed cinder-block buildings with hard pews and musty draperies, the quality of singing was a function of the distance of the congregation from a population center and the ability of scarce sopranos to outsing what my father called the "screen-door altos" (that's what they sounded like) on any given Sunday.

The songs we sang there were "low church" at best, many of them Stamps-Baxter arrangements with melodies and rhythms that sounded just as appropriate for a traveling carnival or vaudeville show.

If the skies above you are gray, you are feeling so blue.
If your cares and burdens seem great, all the whole day through . . .

As one old brother used to say, "If you don't know the tune, just move your lips and tap your foot."

There's a silver lining that shines in the heavenly land.
Look by faith and see it, my friend, trust in his promises grand.

But even though it wasn't always wonderful, it was joyful noise in the literal sense, heartfelt, and I enjoyed it immensely.

Trouble was, the combination of sour notes and Southerners' butchered diction often resulted in my misunderstanding what was being sung. Frequently, what I thought to be the words of some of the songs wasn't always what was printed in the hymnal.

I had several favorites—some funny, some sad, some downright mystifying.

The animal songs were the best. First there was "Gladly, the Cross-eyed Bear." I was ten years old before I realized that it was "Gladly the Cross I'd Bear" and had nothing to do with a dyslexic grizzly. I'd also missed the mark with "Lead On, O King Eternal." Sounded like "kinky turtle" to me.

There was also that line from "Silent Night": "Round John Virgin, mother and child." Who was Round John? I thought. Why was he never pictured with mother and child in the nativity scenes on Christmas cards?

In fact, a handful of songs referred to folks I'd never studied in Sunday school, and I wondered who they were. Shirley Goodness, for example. Why was she going to follow me all the days of my life? Or that guy Andy: "Andy walks with me, Andy talks with me." And Irby in the song "God Will Take Care of You": "Be not dismayed what Irby tied, God will take care of you. . . ." Or " 'Tis Midnight and on Olive's Brow."

I watched the Popeye cartoons almost as religiously as I attended church, and I just couldn't see a connection.

Then there were the sad songs, those that conjured up images that worried my young mind. I felt sorry for the dumb brother who was planting the king's garden in the song "Are You Sowing the Seed of the King, Dumb Brother?" I got in trouble for calling my sister dumb. So, why did we sing it at church?

Or "All hail the power of Jesus' name, let angels' prostrate fall." I didn't know what a prostrate was, but my grandaddy had been in the hospital with his, and I figured it had to be just as painful for the angels.

To this day, I can't help but smile when I hear other songs whose words or titles I somehow managed to get right, but which nevertheless made a striking impression on me.

For instance, "Let Us Break Bread Together on Our Knees," I imagined my father whomping a big ole baguette across his leg and serving it 'round to the family. It was years before I realized that "on our knees" referred to the penitent stance of the believer, not the surface on which the loaf was to be broken.

Then there was the second verse of "Come, Thou Fount of Every Blessing": "Here I raise my Ebenezer, hither by thy help I'm come." I was prepared to raise my Ebenezer with the best of them, even though I wasn't exactly sure what-all it entailed.

And I still grin mischievously when I hear "How Firm a Foundation," despite the fact that it's a lovely, moving old anthem. It's my grandmother's fault. From what I could understand, her foundation was something she wore under her dress on Sundays; I could recall many an afternoon on the way home from church hearing her comment on how un-comfortable her foundation was and how glad she'd be to get out of it. As a little boy, I simply could not imagine why we sang about it from time to time at church—but I knew that if "firm" meant "uncomfortable," MaMa could commiserate.

When I was a child, I understood as a child, but when I be-came a man, I put away childish things. Those lyrics that once were funny or troubling or confusing now comfort and up-lift. The songs are the same, but their meanings now are deeper, dearer, clearer. I remember Shirley Goodness, but I sing "surely goodness and mercy will follow me all the days, all the days of my life."

That's not to say I can't still get a chuckle from an ill-timed church song. Not so long ago I was visiting a small congrega-tion, when the song leader announced the page number of the hymn to be sung just before the minister's sermon. The title? "Ready to Suffer." Let's just say it was an appropriate selection. . . .

The Heretic

————— ◆ —————

MY little girl, Claire, is a heretic—a twenty-month-old tod-
dling disgrace to her Southern roots. Either that or she's
going through a phase.

To my personal chagrin, and to her mother's frustration—
no, more than that—to her mother's downright fury, Claire
won't eat meat.

And that's not all she won't eat. But it just so happens that
meat is the only thing she consistently won't eat—hot dogs
and bologna being the only exceptions, and to say those are
meat is a stretch.

The fact is, there's no consistency to Claire's palate. One
day she'll inhale her SpaghettiOs and butter beans; the next
day she gags on them, and out of her little Betty Boop mouth
they tumble onto her bib in unappetizing, predigested clumps.
Ditto peas, green beans, carrots, even cheese on occasion.
Now whoever heard of a child who wouldn't eat cheese? And
whoever heard of a Southern child who won't eat meat?

My wife, Karen, is merely aggravated by it. I, on the other
hand, feeling the burden of my Southern heritage, am
ashamed . . . and maybe a wee bit melodramatic.

I mean, I can handle her disdain for carrots. I don't like

'em either. But meat? The centerpiece, the *sine qua non,* of the Southern sideboard? It's heresy!

If you grew up in the South, you know what I mean. Meat is to a Southern dinner table what Tang once was to astronauts, what executive privilege is to the Clinton White House, what Kathie Lee is to Regis—that is, essential.

Need some proof? Imagine having the preacher for Sunday lunch and serving him a vegetable plate. Ain't gonna happen. Or say you need to eat on the run, what would you grab: a fistful of mashed potatoes or a cold drumstick? And have you ever driven down a state highway in Alabama and seen a billboard that said EAT MORE BROCCOLI? Of course not. Those signs say EAT MORE BEEF, and they've been around all my life.

Southerners revere animal flesh, can plan entire family gatherings around a loin of beef or a succulent turkey bird or a platter of fried chicken or a side of pork ribs or a crackling pot of greasy catfish or a cloved ham or some barbecued venison. Heck, we can even build a get-together around a coupla squirrels cooked up crisp, which, as any good Southerner knows, taste like chicken.

In fact, those of us blessed enough to be reared by Southern mommas and grandmamas of considerable culinary skill are preconditioned to believe there's no such thing as breakfast without sausage and bacon, dinner without fried chicken or pork chops or pot roast, and supper without meat loaf or salmon croquettes or leftover any-of-the-aforementioned. As my father would say, a meal without meat is just a snack. And, I'm afraid he might add, a granddaughter who won't eat meat is . . . a considerable disappointment.

It's this cultural milieu against which my Claire is apparently rebelling.

We've tried everything: giving it to her straight, and grinding it up (presuming briefly and incorrectly that difficulty with chewing was the problem). We've tried mixing it with other things, only to find that on a forkful of English peas, chicken stands out like a sore thumb. We even disguised it in a gob of macaroni and cheese. She saw through that, so we resorted to begging and bribing. It didn't work, but she enjoyed the spectacle immensely. She's just too young to understand about the starving children in Asia.

So now my wife is inching toward tough love: the "eat this or go hungry" approach. Meanwhile, I find myself fixated on the social implications of it all. Claire's dirty little secret will force us to make some adjustments.

With both sets of Claire's great-grandparents, we'll have to keep her "in the closet," so to speak, scheduling short visits with them between meals, in hopes of hiding my daughter's shameful aversion.

And any church dinners on the grounds are probably out of the question, since Claire won't eat the standard potluck fare of poppy-seed chicken or meat loaf. We've considered asking for prayer.

And from here on out, any dinner invitation we get will—if it includes Claire—have to be BYOB (bring your own bologna).

So I'm bracing myself for the opprobrium and ostracism of our Southern friends and neighbors. Meantime, Karen is looking for a support group. She's not sure which is worse—Claire's finicky eating or my theatrical response to it.

"At least Claire may grow out of her phase," Karen says. "You, on the other hand, are beyond help."

Extraordinarily Normal

———— ◆ ————

I

IF you ever find yourself in Florence, Alabama, on the north side of town, and happen to drive down Patsy Drive, the house marked 118 probably won't catch your eye. A tasteful, sixties-style, single-story home of dark, rough wood and straight lines, it's hardly distinguishable from the others on this very middle-class street.

The couple who built it more than thirty years ago still lives there with their children.

The two of them met in college. Bill and Barbara. He was a true Renaissance man—painter, pilot, musician, and aspiring architect; she—a Southern belle from Walker County, smart and pretty, the eldest of five, and the family's first ever to go to college—would become a teacher. They graduated, married, built their house, and began to talk about a future with children. Definitely with children.

Getting pregnant was difficult, and only when they were about to give up did Barbara learn that she was finally expecting. A daughter, Marla, was born in 1964. A son, Michael, followed four years later.

The kids grew, and life unrolled before them, up and down, through and around, an interesting ride. There were memorable events, precious moments—baptisms; the time Mike, an enthusiastic Crimson Tide fan, got to meet Coach Paul "Bear" Bryant; the week the family spent in Hawaii— good times. There were struggles, too, of course—still are— but everyone has 'em, and they're normal, to be endured. That's how Bill and Barbara see it.

I I

MOST mornings now Barbara awakes first, early, at five A.M. or so. She gets up, makes coffee, awakens Bill. He gets the kids up while she showers and readies herself for work. They both like their jobs. After thirty years in the classroom, she's now an elementary school principal, and a good one, the re-cipient of several awards and much respect from her peers. He's an architect with a distinguished firm downtown, and the banks and churches and parks he's designed grace Flo-rence's landscape like well-chosen words in an eloquent homily. These days, he has little time to paint or play his clar-inet or fly as he once did. Busy with other things, but . . . that's normal.

She leaves for work by seven. He departs when the sitter arrives, sometimes pausing to speak to his neighbor before he pulls out of the driveway. In this close-knit community, the neighbors know each other, watch out for each other.

Bill and Barbara both are home from work by five to re-lieve the sitter and start the night's tasks. Dinner. Baths for the kids. The end to a typical day. The evening slips away and it's

eleven o'clock. Bedtime then, to rest before starting it all
again early the next morning.

If they can rest, that is. If Mike's breathing is normal, if
Marla's blood sugar is regulated, if Mike's feet aren't bother-
ing him, if Marla's circulation is okay, if neither of them need
attention during the night. For Bill and Barbara, resting is a
challenge. Carefree sleep is hard to come by.

After twenty years or more, they're used to it, but familiar-
ity doesn't make it any easier to endure. The only thing predictable is that conditions will decline. They're used to things
getting worse, slowly—thankfully slowly, horribly slowly.
They watch their children wither before them, year after
year, and Bill and Barbara just endure. What else is there to
do?

Because for all the appearance of normalcy, my uncle Bill
and aunt Barbara aren't normal any more than their two special children are normal. But normal to them is the life they
know, the routine—a routine that to anyone else would be
extraordinary.

I I I

WHEN we were children, we knew something was different
about Mike and Marla. Physically, they couldn't keep up.
While the rest of us—a boisterous, self-confident pack of a
half dozen cousins—would run and jump like wild Indians
across the hills and hollows of PaPa's farm, they could not.

When they were very small, there was no reason to suspect
anything was wrong. They grew, learned to walk, rode tricy-
cles, did all the things children eventually learn to do. Per-

fectly normal. Then their parents began to notice a persistent clumsiness, a decline in dexterity. Instead of becoming more sure-footed, their coordination seemed to be ebbing. By the time Mike was four years old and Marla eight, it was apparent that this was more than an awkward phase for the two of them.

Doctors were visited. Specialists sent for. Tests were run. And Mike and Marla were diagnosed with Frederick's ataxia, a very rare genetic disorder that causes the muscles to deteriorate. By some fluke of chance and timing and DNA, both my aunt and uncle carried the recessive gene that resulted in their children's disease.

I V

I was too young to recall how Aunt Barbara and Uncle Bill handled the news of their children's illness, how they coped with its onslaught, how it felt to purchase the first wheelchairs, what it was like to find their children mentally alert but physically less and less able to dress and care for themselves.

I imagine they experienced the normal human emotions—the blaming of themselves, the shaking of clenched fists at fate, the questioning through anguished tears. "Please God, help us understand! Why? Why? Why?"

In His own way, silently, God answered. He answered with family and friends who supported, who prayed, who cheered. He answered with Rosie, the housekeeper who right up to her dying day loved and cared for Mike and Marla as if they were her own. He answered with a church that once collected enough money to buy the family a van completely outfitted for the special needs of Mike and Marla. He answered with neighbors who can be at the back door in a matter of seconds when my aunt and uncle need them. Most of all, He answered by helping Uncle Bill and Aunt Barbara understand that God can make good out of the worst of circumstances.

V

THEY didn't set out to be role models, any more than Marla and Mike did. Didn't mean to show inordinate courage and determination and tenacity and grace. But in living extraordinary lives under difficult circumstances, they're enabling others to see their God. And for them, that's . . . normal.

Home Cooking and World Peace

————— ♦ —————

MY friend Kent is on a fitness kick. He called me the other day from Charlotte to tell me about it.

Seems he's going down to the gym three or four days a week to be pushed and prodded and generally tortured by a personal trainer, all in the name of better health.

He's lost twenty-five pounds already. Says he's eating better, too. Not really eating "healthy," as in eating stuff fit only for rabbits and those with colon disorders, but eating less while still eating the stuff he likes.

He says his diet has returned to its roots, to the home cooking he grew up on, and he says it's done as much to improve his mental health as it has to reduce his waistline.

"It's amazing what a good helping of mashed potatoes, light on the gravy, will do for your disposition," he says. "Or turnip greens. Or a corn muffin. I can eat at the Cupboard two or three times a week, and my whole outlook improves. I sleep better. My wife says I'm easier to live with."

Now, for you who are uninitiated, the Cupboard is a Charlotte, North Carolina, landmark, renowned for its country-style steak and home-style vegetables and cream pies. Eating there brings to my mind Nietzsche, who said something to the effect of, "That which doesn't clog our arteries makes us stronger."

That's Kent's philosophy, at least. Which has set him to thinking about . . . world peace.

"I'm convinced that nations are made or broken by what they eat," says Kent. "Food is much more influential in human relations than most folks think," he adds matter-of-factly.

"Take the Swiss, for instance. What do you think of when you think of Switzerland?" he asks me. It takes me a second to erase the image of Julie Andrews and the von Trapp family singers from my mind.

"Well, they're neutral."

"Exactly!" he says with the fervor of a new convert. "The Swiss haven't fought anybody since they lost to France in the early eighteenth century in It'ly." (Kent is a history buff, by the way.) "Now I maintain that they got down there to It'ly, tasted some of that pasta and prosciutto and focaccia, and there on the spot decided to 'make lunch, not war.' "

"Ah," I say, nodding. This entire conversation is beginning to sound uncomfortably like a bad episode of *Seinfeld*.

Kent continues. "The Swiss are a peace-loving people."

Either that, I think to myself, or like bachelors of a certain age, they just can't make a commitment.

"And you know why they love peace?" Kent asks. "It's the food they eat."

"Huh?"

He persists. "Swiss steak. Swiss cheese. Chocolate and cocoa—that Swiss Miss stuff."

"And don't forget Swiss cake rolls," I interject irreverently. "You know, those little plastic-wrapped, chocolate-covered cakes found on the snack aisle at your local supermarket."

"Nah," says Kent without a trace of irony. "Those are Little Debbies. They're made in Chattanooga.

"But imagine," he continues dreamily, "if more folks took the time to sit down and eat modest portions of good food, wouldn't this be a better world?"

I ponder that one for a minute, envisioning a potluck supper club for the brotherhood of mankind.

"Sure it would!" Kent says, answering his own question. "And you know what I think?" He lowers his voice to a near whisper. "I think Southern home cooking is the way to go."

"Huh?"

"I think the cure for what ails America—heck, the world for that matter—is lunch at the Cupboard. And maybe a little exercise."

"What do you mean?" I ask.

"Take Bob Dole for instance. That man needs some collard greens. Some good ole sweet greasy collard greens. 'Twould do wonders for his disposition."

"And Bill Clinton?" I ask.

"Vegetable plate. The man needs to learn to make hard choices. Carrots. Field peas. Asparagus. Maybe some squash casserole. And a biscuit."

"No pie?" I ask.

"No pie," says Kent.

"Okay . . . Alfonse D'Amato."

"Hog jowl."

"Dan Quayle."

"Liver and onions. It's brain food, you know."

"Okay . . . Pat Buchanan," I say, throwing down the gauntlet.

"Easy," says Kent. "But not American. Something German. Bratwurst and sauerkraut.

"You see what I mean?" he continues. "Imagine the implications for mankind. Look at Northern Ireland. I say you sit those folks down over a plate of chicken and dumplings and blackberry cobbler and there's no way they can be disagreeable. Or Bosnia. Nothing some fried chicken and coconut cream pie can't cure. China? Invite 'em to a fish fry. We'll be friends again in no time."

"I see what you mean," I say.

"And if everyone followed those new serving-size suggestions from the FDA, they'd all feel better and lose weight, too," says Kent.

No, I think to myself, they'd starve to death.

"Well," says Kent, "time for lunch. Gotta run."

"Later," I say, and hang up, visions of fried chicken and new potatoes and peach cobbler simmering in my head. I feel healthier already.

Sarah Palmer

———— ◆ ————

AMONG freshmen at the small Alabama liberal arts college I attended, Sarah Palmer's eccentricities were legendary.

"She plays classical music in her classes!" said my roommate. "You know, Vivaldi and Moze-art, that stuff."

But for me, a product of Alabama's public schools at a time when budget proration had displaced liberal arts—and practically everything else, for that matter—the thought of a college English class complemented by Vivaldi (whoever that was) seemed truly exotic.

It would be another two years before I got around to experiencing Sarah Palmer firsthand. I was a finance major who had chosen an English minor.

"A good combination for getting a job," the dean of business had gushed.

"It's certainly . . . *practical*," Mrs. Palmer later would sniff.

By my junior year, I was in need of an elective to complete my minor. I chose advanced composition over Chaucer, and on the first day of class found myself in a damp, colorless room in Comer Hall listening to Beethoven hiss and crackle from an ancient phonograph.

This was the domain of Sarah Palmer, doyenne of third-floor Comer, nurturer of countless would-be writers, and collector of things interesting: magazine clippings, furniture, books, admiring pupils—all kinds of things.

I was not exactly sure what to expect. As a freshman, I'd heard the music as I occasionally passed the open door of her classroom. And I'd seen her in the English commons room from time to time, so I knew of her sophisticated sense of style and shrewd eye for a bargain. It was a room she'd furnished almost single-handedly, a comfortable oasis of well-worn antique furnishings, good books, and fresh-cut flowers amid the bland, peeling wallpaper of mildewy old Comer Hall.

On any given day she might be found there in her full, calf-length skirt, stretching up to dust the top of a lovely old mahogany armoire that commanded the room, or standing over a side table arranging forsythia, spirea, and wild hydrangea in a vase—an unpretentious, slightly built, sensibly attired grandmother, her hair in a graying pageboy.

"And how are you?" she'd say, her voice contralto, bassoonlike—not a croak, but not exactly a tinkle either. She would look up from her task for a split second, smiling, as if responding graciously to a greeting I hadn't offered.

I began to suspect that this woman was more than the sum of her parts, that her penchant for flowers and Beethoven and antiques and polite conversation weren't the loose strings of a fraying, eccentric personality, but the threads of gold in a fabric whose entire pattern I could not yet discern. Little did I realize how the coming semester would broaden my view, would serve as a primer for beginning to weave my own fabric.

She arrived for her classes early, in plenty of time to start the phonograph and organize the volumes of handouts for which she was renowned. "I clipped this from *The New Yorker* yesterday—thought someone here might like it," she'd say. Then, without taking a breath, "Isn't it an interesting perspective on euthanasia? And did anyone hear Jesse Jackson's speech at the Democratic convention? Marvelous use of imagery. Well done. Some of you might want to try that. Now . . ." And finally taking a breath, she'd launch into the day's topic, speaking in short, clipped sentences and with staccato diction.

Her teaching style was electric, her face and limbs conductors of the current. No one slept through Mrs. Palmer's class. She was too energetic, too interesting for that. She was baptized with a passion for teaching writing, so that when she lifted the needle on the phonograph and class began, mild-mannered matron became dynamo, whirling dervish–like from well-studied topic to well-chosen example to well-supported criticism, all supplemented by her contagious energy, abundant handouts, and illegible scrawl on the chalkboard. We observed, open-mouthed.

"Do you see it?" she'd inquire over her shoulder as she scribbled hieroglyphics on the board.

"Now you try it," she'd say, turning to peer at us over her black-rimmed half-frame glasses. And so we would.

She would return my essays with her suggestions marked ever so lightly in pencil (so as not to compromise my authorship with her own ideas, I guessed). There would be strike-throughs, arrows indicating where I might want to relocate a sentence, and brief suggestions scratched in the margin.

Her markings served not to rewrite a student's work, but to give us a nudge down a truer path. "You have a good start here," she would write at the top of the page. "Now improve on it." Or "Surprise your reader with interesting details. Make them up if you have to. Remember, sometimes we have to lie to tell the truth."

We always knew when an assignment was imminent. Mrs. Palmer would utter her favorite make-believe word: "Pl'ike." *Pl'ike:* a contraction of "play like," synonym for "pretend."

"Let's pl'ike we're reviewers for *The New York Times Book Review.* Pick a book, read it, and review it."

I chose an autobiography—*Growing Up* by Russell Baker—read it and dutifully wrote my review. Days later, I got my paper back, scribbled lightly upon, with a curious directive jotted across the top: "This is fine work. *Do* something with it."

I had no idea what to *do* with it, but Mrs. Palmer did. She entered it in the annual campus-wide writing competition. I promptly forgot about it until weeks later, when she called me to her cramped office and handed me two envelopes. In one was a check for a hundred dollars. I'd won. And in the other was a short note from Russell Baker himself.

Dear Sarah Palmer,

Thanks for sending me a copy of your student's review of *Growing Up.*

You ought to be proud . . .

I didn't have to pl'ike I was astonished.

As a teacher, Sarah Palmer was no snob when it came to *good* writing; no respecter of persons. If not everyone writes well (and not everyone does), she told us, then those who do should be nurtured and encouraged and should be read and reread. One was just as likely to hear her mention Erma

Bombeck in her lectures as Hemingway or Welty or Faulkner. For the first time, I felt like it was okay to admire Lewis Grizzard, Russell Baker, or George Plimpton.

"What are they, if they're not writers?" she'd say, reminding us not to judge the quality of one's writing by its print medium—if it was printed at all. "Good writing defies categorization. Good writing doesn't have to appear in an anthology to prove its worth. Even a letter to a friend can be a masterpiece," she'd intone.

Her own letters to me, if not masterpieces, certainly are prized possessions. We began corresponding shortly after I graduated, and I've come to look forward to receiving the three or four missives I now get from her each year. I save them all. The challenge is to decipher her handwriting while managing to follow her meandering lines across and around the page. When she runs out of space at the bottom, she starts up the left margin and over the top and back down the other side. And then, in closing, "Are you writing?" she'll scrawl, or "Keep at it!" or "Send me something you've written!"

In Sarah Palmer, I met my match, my mentor, maybe even my muse. She practiced with me what she preached. In me— not only me, but numerous others as well—she saw something worth encouraging, worth coaching, worth reading.

And so I write, not always well, perhaps, but always driven—haunted even—by the expectation of a lady who nurtured my questionable talent and changed my life. "Send me something you've written!"

Far be it from me to let her down.

Making Soup

———— ♦ ————

ANY day now, the late field peas are gonna come in. Corn, too, if it hasn't already. The okra, tender and green and fuzzy, will be ready to cut, and there'll be speckled butter beans to pick and shell, and potatoes to dig.

That's when the phone will ring at certain homes across Alabama and north Georgia, and on the other end of the line, my MaMa, her voice crackling like hot grease in an iron skillet, will say to her daughters and daughters-in-law, "You'uns come on. It's time to make soup."

Then my mother and her sisters and sisters-in-law will load up the dozens of quart Mason jars and canning rings they've been collecting since last winter, and the scarred Tupperware bowls they'll use for looking the beans, plus the vegetable knives, corn cutters, silking brushes, pressure cookers, and the cardboard boxes they've been saving for just this purpose, and they'll point their cars toward a little yellow house on a hill near Parrish, Alabama, toward home, just as they've been doing in early August for as long as I can remember.

Time to make soup.

As a child, I hated soup making, hated the heat and the gnats and the stain the purple-hull peas left on my fingers.

One year, I ate five green apples off PaPa's tree, fully expecting to get a debilitating stomachache that would release me
from my appointed soup-making chores. I did get a debilitating stomachache, but MaMa showed no mercy. She gave me
castor oil and sent me to the porch to shell peas with my
cousins. I wore a path between the porch and the bathroom
that day and still must have shelled a bushel on my own.

At soup-making time, the window of opportunity is short,
and everybody who can walk works. Only at a certain time
in early August are all the requisite vegetables available at the
same time. Sure, you can have cabbage and early peas in June,
but not okra. There are new potatoes in late May, but not
tomatoes. Only in early August do all the vegetables "come
in" just right, and that's soup-making time. MaMa declares
the day—sometimes the third, sometimes the seventh or
tenth or thirteenth, depending on how much rain we've had.

When I was a kid, soup-making day would start before
sunup, before the heat mixed with the heavy, humid air to
make the afternoon insufferable. It was hard work, reserved
for the women and children of the family, for the menfolk
had real jobs. It began with a bumpy ride on the rutted,
eroded path that led over the hill and through the pasture,
verdant and aromatic with cow droppings, and on to the garden—a three-acre stretch of remarkably prolific dirt whose
yield helped sustain our entire extended family through winter after winter.

MaMa would not tolerate dillydallying, and right away, six
or eight cousins would be dispatched in dawn's early light to
rows of peas or butter beans, corn or okra, to pick and to
sweat, not always in that order. The aunts picked, too, faster
than two of us cousins put together, but I preferred to think

of my indenture in malevolent terms, as if we kids were being sent to the pea patch to single-handedly support our respective households.

The dirt would be warm under our bare feet, the fronds of dew-coated johnsongrass and pea vines, cold and slimy as tentacles, twining around our legs. Somehow, I always ended up picking peas despite the fact that I didn't even eat the things. My cousin Anthony got to pull corn, which meant partial shade when the sun came up (he was the oldest). My sister dug peanuts. I got peas. Only my cousin Ginger, who cut okra, had it worse. She'd itch for the rest of the day. At least my wet legs would dry.

By eight in the morning, the picking was done, bushel baskets and coolers and croaker sacks full of fresh corn, peas, cabbage, butter beans, potatoes, tomatoes, cantaloupes, onions, and okra were loaded in the back of PaPa's pickup along with the obligatory watermelon for later, and we'd head for the house. But the work was just beginning.

Next came sorting and assignments. It was always the same. Beans and peas stayed on the patio, where we unfortunate cousins commenced shelling under the shade of a venerable water oak. Corn was taken to the back of the house to be shucked and silked alongside the pasture fence, where the cows would come up and gobble husks right from your hand—or Anthony's hand, I should say (he was the oldest). Okra was taken around to the high front porch, where my aunts found the ancient iron glider there a perfect seat for cutting. Potatoes were peeled and quartered wherever there was a free spot. And tomatoes—the *sine qua non* of vegetable soup—were taken to the kitchen. This was a plum assignment, for whoever got the kitchen got to work with MaMa, got to do soup magic in the large, blue-speckled stewing pots. Whoever got the kitchen got air-conditioning. I never got the kitchen.

So, while we kids shelled and shucked and the less fortunate aunts looked the beans and peas or scraped corn on slender aluminum cutters, MaMa and the anointed daughter inside prepared tomatoes. Preparation, I knew, consisted of putting them in a big pot and juicing them out, but what they did after that is a mystery to me. All I know is that, shortly, the whole house would fill with the smell of cooking tomatoes. It seemed to ooze from the knotty-pine-paneled walls of MaMa's kitchen and whirl over the mahogany Duncan Phyfe table in the dining room, then waft on an all-too-gentle breeze out to the patio, where it offered us inmates a brief respite from the flies and the monotony of shelling. Intoxicated by the aroma, someone would begin to hum a familiar tune, then another would join in, and before long I would be leading aunts and cousins in a rousing chorus of "Kneel at the Cross" or "I'm Henery the Eighth (I Am)" (our repertoire could be rather eclectic).

"Randall Scott!" Mother would screech, peering from the kitchen window, knowing I was the ringleader. "I don't hear any work going on out there!" (I was never sure what work was supposed to sound like, but it apparently could not be done in four-part harmony.)

"Yes, ma'am." I'd sigh.

Shortly—when the tomatoes were juiced out, thick and bubbly in the stewing pots—an aunt would begin to shuttle between the picking, shucking, peeling, cutting stations and the kitchen, gathering up vegetables and delivering them to be mixed into the succulent, tomatoey brine according to MaMa's unwritten recipe.

Then about three in the afternoon, when the mixture was ready, MaMa would call for the Mason jars. This was the final step. In our family, Mason jars have more lives than a cat. A quart jar that began its useful life as a container for green beans might come back the next year full of pear preserves or some of PaPa's honey. The next year, soup maybe. Then sweet pickles or pickled beets. And on and on, until careless hands drop it or it's accidentally thrown out by an unindoctrinated in-law or it's given over to a grandchild as a home for tadpoles or lightning bugs.

Anyway, we'd disgorge the accumulated jars from car trunks and backseats and deliver them to be filled with soup, red and thick and chock-full of the garden's bounty. Lids and rings were placed on the jars, then into the pressure cooker they went, to seal. The jars came out steamy and wet, their contents as red as a hussy's lipstick, to be divvied up, transported home, and stored in the pantry. Some suitable winter evening a few months hence would set us to craving that soupy warmth of summer.

That was how we did it. Still is, for MaMa and her daughters and daughters-in-law. Any day now, the late field peas are gonna come in. Corn, too, if it hasn't already. . . .

Bible Bowl

———— ◆ ————

MY parents had an antidote for sticky July days: church camp. It was an annual summer ritual, as certain as the muggy thickness of a July noontime or the hiss and squeal of well-aimed bottle rockets on the Fourth or the welts left by vampire mosquitoes that preyed on lean, bronze limbs in the relative cool of a July dusk.

In the July doldrums, my parents sent me to church camp. I didn't mind; it was a happenin' place, a page out of the L.L. Bean catalog, except with kudzu and pine trees. There I could cut up and commiserate and devotionalize with a hundred or so other sweaty kids just like me—plus there was swimming.

I'm recalling it all now because, well, for one thing, it's July, and today I'd much rather be canoeing Hargis Lake or even weaving polyester potholders in the crafts hut than preparing for this afternoon's budget meeting. But this July also brings to mind a dubious church camp anniversary, conjures up memories of youthful hubris and a stunning personal failure. It was the year I learned just how closely destruction chases a haughty spirit.

It's been twenty years, and I remember the ignominy of it

like it was yesterday: church camp, July 1977. I was fourteen, between the seventh and eighth grades, and awash in puberty and pimples and self-doubt cloaked in overcompensating extroversion.

Poised there on the edge of young manhood, I planned to take the camp by storm, and by bluffing my way through, to be scintillating and smart and ultimately . . . *Popular.* All it would take, I figured, was for me to triumph in the Bible Bowl, that climactic, nail-biting church camp event, and the chicks, lovely in their stylish green eyeshadow and Farrah Fawcett haircuts, would be all over me.

Bible Bowl was a Bible trivia tournament, a sort of "*Jeopardy* Meets the Minor Prophets," in which our avuncular youth minister, Mr. Blackstone, played the congenial host. We'd been given a list of study questions and answers on Sunday, when we arrived, and were expected to spend any spare moments cramming for Thursday's big event. Resolute, I poured myself into the questions, missing volleyball and canteen to study. I even stayed awake to memorize by dim flashlight the differences between Sadducees and Pharisees long after my bunkmates had already turned in.

By Thursday morning I was ready, and so cocky that my ego could have applied for statehood. What I didn't count on was . . . Marvin Groot. Marvin was—well, not to be cruel, but Marvin was fat. He was flabby and soft, and arrogant to boot. He was also incredibly smart and incredibly obnoxious.

I wasn't exactly a teen idol myself, what with my ill-suited Andy Gibb haircut and husky-size jeans. But if I was a geek, Marvin was, thankfully, geekier. If I was chubby, Marvin was the Pillsbury Doughboy. For an awkward, pubescent period of time, he was my consolation, my solace, the person who made my pimples endurable. Sure, I'm a dweeb, I told myself, but I'm no Marvin Groot.

The preliminaries began on Thursday after lunch. The action centered around a dusty card table on which was placed a primitive, battery-powered gizmo with two lightbulbs on top. From both sides of the gizmo came cords. On the end of each cord was a button. When either button was pushed, the machine let out an unpleasant electronic cough and activated the corresponding lightbulb. Its purpose was to tell the audience which contestant was answering the question. For its day, it was the epitome of high tech. It cast an awesome spell on us, eliminating many a trigger-happy contestant who simply, sheepishly, might keep buzzing the buzzer at all the wrong times, just for the inexplicable feeling of raw power it gave him.

And so by late afternoon, the weak were winnowed out and only the fittest remained. Two of us. I'd made the finals. I smelled victory.

"Attention campers, the final round of Bible Bowl 1977 will commence in five minutes in the mess hall: Scott Brunner"—somewhere, I thought I heard teenage girls cheering—"versus Marvin Groot"—a palpable "eghhh!" went up through the camp.

We met across the dusty table, having each vanquished our own dozen pretenders to the championship. Marvin sat across from me, an expression of bemused indifference on his puffy little face. Not to be intimidated, I smiled sweetly back at him. Fat chance, Fatso, I thought smugly to myself.

"Ladies and Gentlemen, we've reached the final round of Bible Bowl competition, and before you sit our finalists. Now, boys, let's be gentlemen. Remember, it's not whether you win or lose, it's—" The rest of the speech was lost on me as I dreamed of victory, of being hoisted on the shoulders of the other kids and carried to the front of the dinner line amid cheers and adulation. "Let us begin," said Mr. Blackstone.

The questions flew, the buzzers buzzed. One round. Two rounds. Three rounds. Nearing dinnertime, the score was tied. At this point, all it would take was for one of us to miss a question, to choke, and the other would win. And then, in the tie-breaking fourth round, it came.

Said Mr. Blackstone, "Who baptized—"

Ecstatic, I hit the button, cutting Mr. Blackstone off in midsentence. *Ackkkkk!* went my buzzer, and on came my light. I knew this one! I knew it! I knew—

And then I remembered: there were *two* "who baptized?" questions on the study list. I hadn't the slightest idea which one this was. I hadn't waited to hear. Okay, okay, okay, I coached myself, fifty percent chance. It's either "Who baptized Saul?" or "Who baptized the Ethiopian eunuch?" The eunuch. Go with the eunuch.

"Uh . . . would it be . . . Philip the Apostle?" I asked tentatively. For a long second, no one breathed.

Finally: "I'm sorry, Mr. Brunner. Mr. Groot, would you like to hear the rest of the question?"

The rest was a blur. I recall it now, only because . . . well, come to think of it, that budget meeting today doesn't seem so bad after all.

My Neighbor

——— ◆ ———

MY next-door neighbor died this past weekend—came in from an afternoon of yard work, sat down in an easy chair, and died. Heart attack.

I don't know how old he was—sixty or so, I'd guess. I've checked the obituaries in the newspaper every day this week in hopes of finding out, but that's been problematic too, because . . . I don't know his name.

I'm ashamed to admit it, but I've lived next door to the man for two years and I don't even know his name.

I've admired his handiwork in his yard—the immaculate beds of redtips and hollies and flowers and the lush, manicured Saint Augustine grass—but I never asked his name.

I've watched him turn, with his wife's help, a patch of Yazoo clay in his backyard into some lovely tomatoes, but I didn't compliment them.

I've snickered at my wife and her continual annoyance at his summertime habit of plodding around his yard, shirtless, belly hanging over saggy Bermuda shorts and brogans. At those times I noticed the vivid scar on his chest—bypass surgery, I was certain—but I never asked about it. I never said anything at all.

I remember one Saturday last summer how, unsolicited, he saved the day by backing his brand-new, bright red, four-wheel-drive Chevy truck into my low-lying backyard. Then he unfurled the winch on the front of the truck and pulled from axle-deep mud the trailer-load of pine logs my dad and I had managed to get stuck there. I thanked him profusely. Offered him a glass of iced tea. But I didn't think to ask his name.

This summer I saw him, evening after evening, wobbling up and down the street in front of his house and mine, picking up Styrofoam to-go boxes covered with ants and the glutinous residue of hot lunch from the Jitney. I saw him gather from the street the paper Burger King bags and variously labeled cigarette cartons, all blown across from the new home construction site across the street from us. I heard him cursing under his breath the subcontractors who could be so shiftless as to leave their trash lying about. But I didn't stop him to get acquainted.

And one evening just last week, as I wrestled in the grass with my little girl, Claire, in our front yard, he walked by, paused, held out a handful of nails and staples he'd just collected from the street between his driveway and mine. I almost smiled at the single-word epithet he used to describe a home builder who would allow such a mess to be hurled into the street around his construction site. I agreed with his assessment, but I didn't extend my hand and say, "I'm Scott, by the way. I don't know that we've ever introduced ourselves." Instead I let him walk on, muttering to himself.

And so, since his passing, I've had to rely on other neighbors for information about him, the funeral, his family, and what can be done for them at this difficult time.

And I'm truly ashamed. Ashamed that I've used my electronic garage-door opener as a door closer, a tool for insulating me and my family from the chore of maintaining relationships with people whom I've presumed I have nothing in common with. I'm ashamed that I've spent more time cultivating my azaleas and zinnias than I have cultivating good relations with my next-door neighbor. And I'm ashamed I haven't been more like my parents. Within a week of those folks moving in two years ago, Mom would have delivered a fresh pound cake to the newcomers and Dad would have trotted over to admire the guy's lawn mower and chat for a spell.

I was taught to be that way, too. Growing up, when someone on our little street passed away, Mom would dispatch my sister and me to circle the neighborhood with a battered envelope, taking contributions for flowers for the deceased and helping organize who would take which casserole to the grieving family.

I wonder now how I grew from that little boy into a man who's poured his energies into his work community and church community and even an Internet community—and overlooked the nameless neighbor at his own back fence.

Little Green Apples

———— ◆ ————

EARLY this morning, when my grandmother went to gather apples, the legacy was the furthest thing from her mind. She was just trying to get out there before the birds and squirrels discovered the ripe, sour apples that had hit the ground in the night, before diligent ants commandeered the fallen fruit and deprived us of the fried apple pies that she'll surely make before the day is over.

So she awakened at sunup, pulled on a threadbare pink housecoat and her slippers, and scurried (as best a plump, arthritic eighty-year-old woman can scurry) down the hill to the pasture fence, where the old apple tree has stood for fifty years or more, diminutive, noble, and wizened. As she placed bruised apples in a plastic bag from the Piggly Wiggly, she might have remembered the story, the legend of this apple tree, but I doubt it. She was more concerned with her chore and with getting back to the house to put on some coffee for PaPa.

But I'm certain she knows the story, for she's the one who told it to me as a child: how this variety of apple has been in the family for generations; how it's a graft from a tree that grew at PaPa's old homeplace when he was a boy; how that old tree was itself a graft of a graft that ancestors had brought from Scotland sometime in the previous century.

"Hit's just uh ole sour apple," she'd told me. "Don't have a name, far's I know."

Later on, my uncle, her son, embellished the story, recalling the words of an unnamed great-grandrelative who, years earlier, perhaps on his deathbed even, had whispered the haunting blessing that came with those family apples: "The best apple tree to have," the old relative recalled being told by some otherwise forgotten patriarch years earlier. "Hardy enough to endure freeze or drought or disease that will kill off other varieties."

"No matter what," the old codger wheezed dramatically to my uncle, "that tree will always yield enough apples to take care of the family."

That's the story I was told, at least, and since the old apple tree has yet to let us down, I choose to believe it.

But when it's first light and already muggy and there's biscuits yet to be rolled out and bacon to be fried and there you stand down by the pasture fence in your housecoat, in plain view of the bleary-eyed coal miners and power-plant workers who sip strong coffee in cracked, stained mugs as they ease their battered pickups down Liberty Hill Road toward the morning shift—when that's the situation, a body tends to wanna get on with it and skip the sublime details.

So I'm guessing MaMa didn't take time to reflect much, not even on the sheer ugliness of the fruit she was scooping up, each apple a freckled stepchild, green-gold and dappled with gray-bronze splotches that look like liver spots on a palsied hand. She knows, I suppose, as it is with most things, the beauty is inside.

Late morning, when the heat of the day had set in, she peeled and sliced the fruit, two or three days' worth, and put them out to dry in the incandescent August sun. This is itself a family tradition—the drying of those sour apples on corrugated tin sheets that are laid across PaPa's old aluminum boat, and later, her performing the curious alchemy that blends dried apples and secret spices inside a delicate crust to make fried pies.

And MaMa's fried apple pies simply are too good for lowly prose. The secret, of course, is in the apples. Those sour, old, legendary apples.

And right about now, as the coal miners and power-plant workers pass back by on their way home to supper, there are hot fried pies laid out like bricks on saucers on MaMa's kitchen windowsill, and down the hill by the pasture fence, newly ripened apples, ready to fall, cling precariously to the branches, awaiting the dark.

Just Do It

———— ◆ ————

IN west central Alabama, near the Mississippi state line, there's a little town named after—or named before; I'm not sure—Motor City, USA. But it's not called Detroit, like that third-world metropolis of unions, Yankees, and violent crime in Michigan. It's *Dee*-troit. *Dee*-troit, Alabama.

Growing up in the Heart of Dixie, I thought we had the monopoly on oddly named places and oddly pronounced place names. I grew up hearing of funny-sounding places like Talladega and Tallapoosa and Eastaboga and Opp and Slapout and Intercourse (yes, there's an Intercourse, Alabama. I've always said that someday I want to write a travel guide about my home state and call it *Oh, to Be in Intercourse Now That Spring Is Here*). There's also Mobile (Mo-*bill,* not Moble or Mo-*byle,* as you'd think) and Remlap (that's Palmer spelled backward) and Clio (not Cleo), where George Wallace was from.

But since moving to Mississippi a couple of years ago, I've learned that Alabama ain't got nothin' on the Magnolia State when it comes to funny-named towns and vernacular pronunciations. Take for instance the fair town of Chunky, in east central Mississippi. It's gotta be tough being from there.

How'd you like to be the Chunky mayor? Or worse, a Chunky cheerleader?

Add to that quite an assortment of Indian and ethnic and odd towns and counties: Pascagoula, Nitta Yuma, Okolona, Itta Bena, Pontotoc, Itawamba, Kosciusko, Coahoma, Pelahatchie. Also, Duck Hill, Hot Coffee, Iuka, and of course, Bovina, where folks have to watch where they step.

But while Nitta Yuma and Chunky are pretty unusual-sounding names for places, they're not nearly as interesting as the way Mississippians pronounce what should be fairly normal-sounding place names, but aren't. The fact is, an Alabama accent won't get you very far over here. To get by, you have to have a grasp of the inscrutable rules of Mississippi inflection and pronunciation.

I learned this the first time my attorney-friend Chuck asked me to meet him at Frank's Place in Jackson for lunch shortly after I moved to town. "I think I know where that is," I told Chuck. "Don't I turn off State Street onto Amity . . . ?"

"Amity?" He laughed. "Spell that."

I was puzzled. "A-M-I-T-E. Amity. I 'spect it's French or Cajun."

"It could be Lithuanian for all folks around here know," Chuck said. "We say 'Amitt.' Amitt Street. Amitt County."

Of course, Chuck has no right to throw stones. A reformed Yankee, his family moved to Mississippi from Illinois when he was in grade school, to a little town in the northeast corner of the state. The cracks show in that imitation Southern facade of his when he slips up and tells folks he's from Co-*rinth*. He may be the only person in the state who says it that way. "Never heard of it," someone'll say. "Now, I got a cousin in *Co*-rinth. 'S 'at anywhere near where you're from?"

Over here, forget the spelling. Pronunciation is everything. Say it wrong and you've marked yourself as a carpetbagger. I've learned quickly that the best way to spot an outsider is simply to show 'em a map and ask 'em to tell you what county the University of Mississippi is located in. If they say Lah-fee-*ette,* you've got an interloper on your hands. Most Mississippians—even MSU graduates—know it's La-*fay*-ette.

There are even regional pronunciations within the state. Get north of Highway 82, and the *o*'s and *i*'s start to sound like *a*'s. How in the world do you get Belzona out of B-E-L-Z-O-N-I? That's Belzonee, isn't it? Or Hernand*a,* up in DeSot*a* County, two places apparently named for that legendary Spanish explorer . . . Hernand*a* de Sot*a.*

Then there's *Olive* Branch, only it's not *Olive* Branch, it's Olive *Branch*—emphasis on the Branch. I don't know why. Seems like it would be the other way around, since I suspect branches (that's Southern-speak for a small crick, by the way) are slightly more abundant than olives up there; hence the need for emphasizing which branch rather than which olive. But that's not how the locals say it: "Let's go inta Olive *Branch* and get a cold drank."

Another one that defies reason is Bogue Chitto (Boga Chitta). I just don't get it. They might as well have spelled out Mononucleosis on the city limits sign and called it Boga Chitta, 'cause how it's spelled and how it's pronounced could just as well be two different languages.

And then there's D'Lo. D'Lo, Mississippi. Just recently I learned the story—well, *a* story—of how D'Lo got its name. Seems that the woods in and around D'Lo are fairly low-lying, and when the area was first settled, it was prone to flooding. Come a big spring rain, folks'd have to load up their wagons and head for higher ground. Their general complaint was that the land down there was—pardon my French, here—"too damn low." (You see where this is going, doncha?) The effect of years of fleeing rising floodwaters was that the area came to be known by that epithet. Naturally, it later was shortened to D'Lo, I s'pose so that the local girls could tell folks where they lived without embarrassing themselves or their mommas.

And that's it, except for It—I-T—It, Mississippi. It's a real place, located in Copiah County, south of Hazelhurst. Sure, It's small, but for the folks who live there, It's home. And like I always say, when you can't be in Intercourse (Alabama, that is), just do It.

There She Is . . .

————— ◆ —————

THIS Saturday night when Miss Mississippi walks down that runway during the parade of states in Atlantic City, it'll mark the official end to another glorious climacteric in the South: pageant season 1998.

Come Sunday, there'll be a new Miss America, the signal for disappointed-but-nevertheless-doting mommas of local pageant finalists from Durham to Dallas to carefully pack away the gowns, fire batons, tap shoes, ventriloquist dummies, and I don't know what-all until next spring, when the local preliminaries start up again. Another season, another reason for wearing sequins. . . .

There'll be football to occupy our attention during the intervening months, but even football can't always dish up the nail-biting melodrama or the spectacle of a good ole-fashioned beauty pageant. Even though that's not what they're called anymore.

These days, they're *scholarship* pageants, which is okay, I guess, because it suggests that there's now room for extraordinarily talented, eminently intelligent but nevertheless average-looking young women to compete for the crown, the college money, and the lifetime supply of Kraft macaroni and cheese (or whatever it is). The aim, apparently, is to place less emphasis on appearance and more on substance, an updating of that old adage about the fleetingness of good looks: "Beauty is only skin deep, but scholarship goes all the way to the bone."

Still, any way you look at it, this is spin at its most transparent. Anytime you put a bunch of shapely, young females in swimsuits—bikinis, even—and parade 'em in front of a rowdy crowd to be judged like prize sows at the state fair, ain't nobody thinkin' 'bout what's this one's IQ and how 'bout the grade-point average on that one. It's a beauty contest, plain and simple.

But we Southerners don't mind the euphemistic subterfuge. They could call it the Ballet Russe and we'd still tune in to see our Miss Mississippi.

I mean that generically . . . sort of. Not all Southerners start the evening cheering for Miss Mississippi, but they might as well. After all, she is the apotheosis of beauty queens, the one to bet on, the one most often left standing when those other sweet Southern girls have botched their interview questions. Granted, Miss Alabama or Florida or South Carolina may get the nod every now and again, but they all bow to the winning tradition that is Miss Mississippi.

Her stats are impressive: a dazzling four Miss America titlists (the names of whom many Mississippians know by heart), plus countless first or second or third runners-up, and seldom a year without at least a Top 10 finish. In a region better known for its failures, Miss Mississippi represents success.

That explains why she's royalty in her home state, the kind of royalty you never tire of, since there's a fresh, friendly face every year. And she's so darn accessible: sooner or later you're bound to run into her down at the Wal-Mart on a Saturday morning, wearing her tiara and autographing eight-by-ten glossies for the homefolks.

Besides, we knew this gal when she didn't have a crown to croon in, when she was just some little ole preliminary winner, Miss Goosepond Colony or Miss Dixie Belle maybe, come to town, valise in hand, to strut her stuff before the television cameras and capacity crowd at the Vicksburg Convention Center, where Miss Mississippi is broadcast live statewide every June. Another pretty face in another pretty crowd.

And yet, amid all those TV commercials for pageant dresses, she caught our eye, and in an instant we knew, the judges knew, this was the one; knew that this dear, sweet, fair-haired, voluptuous child was sent to us, as Queen Esther in the Bible, for such a time as this. Okay, so her song needed work and the hair was a little poofy and yellow really wasn't her color. Didn't matter. We *knew.*

Then, over the summer, we watched her blossom under the training of handlers who softened her look, convinced her to pick a song more suitable to her vocal range, grilled her on El Niño and Kenneth Starr and human rights abuses in China so that she'd be up to speed for that Atlantic City interview.

Suddenly, in a promotional spread in last week's newspaper, we saw before us our very own Eliza Doolittle. Now, having grown accustomed to her face, how can we not adore her?

We love our Miss Mississippi, for she symbolizes the best in us, all that we are collectively and yet aren't—cannot ever be—individually. After all, she has a crown. She alone, in her radiance and grace, with dewy eyes, sinewy limbs, and gentle drawl, is vindication enough for the century-old losses with which our region continues to grapple, so we anoint her year after year after year with rhinestone tiara and whisk her off to Atlantic City to show those Yankees a thing or two.

So this Saturday night, everything we Southerners know about honor and tradition and loss—the burden of Southern history, if you will—we'll put on the line, or rather the runway, understanding that, in this epic contest, fate is seldom unkind to Southerners, and Miss Mississippi is the queen of the South.

On that sequin-studded Atlantic City battlefield, history just may be on our side.

Labor Day

◆

THE pine straw has begun to fall on my driveway, and a few brightly colored sweet gum leaves—timid wraiths, curled and brittle—fidget impatiently at the foot of the front steps, as if waiting for an invitation in.

Other than that, you'd not suspect that September and Labor Day are here.

After all, the crape myrtles are yet a spectacle, the ginger lilies still preen fragrantly in the backyard, and for my zinnias these are glory days. The temperature still simmers around ninety, and the air is heavy and thick.

Yet summer and fall have begun their perennial joust for supremacy. Though the conclusion is foregone, summer (at least here in the South) refuses to go gently, overstaying its welcome, confusing our seasonal sensibilities and confounding our fall wardrobes.

So to make the break clean—in our minds at least—there comes Labor Day. It's an artificial, commercialized break, of course, a break of convenience, the punctuating ellipsis at the end of a steamy, unfinished summer sentence—*dot, dot, dot*—as if to tell us, "there's a bit more summer to come, but . . ."

That's Labor Day: the somewhat arbitrary dividing line between easygoing summer and sterner autumn.

Labor Day steals in, mildly schizophrenic, the Woody Allen of holidays, ambivalently bearing mixed news. "Enjoy it while you can," it tells us. "Have a fling, for tomorrow you die." Labor Day exhorts the virgins (and everyone else) to make the most of time. Its whispered message is serious. "Put away your white shoes; vacation's over. Now get back to work, back to class, back to reality. Oh, and you may want to give yourself a few extra minutes, driving in: there's school traffic to contend with."

Labor Day, in its own way, allows us those few extra minutes, that bit of extra time we need to catch up and readjust after a summer spent wasting away in Margaritaville or sunning at the lake or reading in a hammock in the backyard.

Despite that, it's an odd sort of holiday, coming at an odd time. Here, at the end of vacation season, we're handed another vacation day, and we're not exactly sure what to do with it. Should we spend it partying or simply catching our breath? Just what's this day all about, anyway?

Not feeling our own labors worthy of honoring with an oddly timed day off, we tend to assign substitute purposes to Labor Day based on whatever it is we happen to need at the time. In that sense, it becomes a holiday without portfolio—a utility day, adaptable, suitable for any cause or occasion.

On Labor Day, we get around to celebrating those things that, because of geographic proximity or work commitments or ball schedules or little Emily's ballet recital, we just didn't—or won't—get around to in the correct season. In my family we've co-opted Labor Day for marking noteworthy but ill-timed anniversaries (my grandparents' sixtieth), or celebrating family reunions (the Texas cousins we'd never met were in town), and even as a make-up date for those Independence Day fireworks (it rained on the Fourth).

This Labor Day weekend, nearly four months early, we're gathering to mark my grandmother's eightieth birthday with a party in north Alabama. For seventy-nine years she's been saddled with a December 27 birthday that, despite our best efforts, always gets lost in the Christmas bustle. This year's milestone demands more attention, however, and, well . . . what about Labor Day?

It's her fling all right, and ours: the last homemade ice cream of the year, the last watermelon cutting, the last fresh vegetables, the last water-ski run on the lake, the last get-together before Thanksgiving.

Come Tuesday, for all intents and purposes, my grandmother will be eighty, it'll be autumn . . . and I'll need to sweep my driveway.

Twins

———— ◆ ————

I was standing at the kitchen counter the other day jotting something in my Day-Timer when my wife, Karen, came home from the doctor. She handed me a grainy, fax-paper photograph of something that looked like two fuzzy bug splats on a dirty windshield and held up two fingers.

"What?" I asked, confused by the picture and hoping that the fingers meant "Peace" or maybe she needed two on the fifty for the Auburn-Florida game.

She pointed to the ultrasound image she'd handed me. I glanced back at it and—surprise! panic!—there, on that crinkly paper, were the next twenty or so years of my life. BABY A and BABY B, the nurse had marked them—two luminescent butter beans in a darkened sonographic pod.

She might as well have handed me a double anchor with diapers on it. I stood there like Bambi in headlights. For a few long seconds, my eyes alternated between the picture in my hand and Karen's face, and I wondered if the goofy, loving look I was wearing at all betrayed the sick feeling in my stomach. I've been in shock ever since.

It's not that we weren't hoping for another child. With our

daughter, Claire, nearing her second birthday, the timing seemed just about right. I even wanted three children. Eventually. But *one at a time,* please. This wasn't at all what I'd planned. And there was the rub: my plan.

Like a modern-day Dolly Levi, I have always been a person who arranges things, so to speak—at least the things in my little life. I'm an inveterate organizer, a planner. Always have been. By the time I was twenty-one, I had my life laid out in well-ordered little parcels on the landscape of my existence, had distilled my days down to a set of what I naively thought were perfectly predictable eventualities. In planning, I just knew I could weed out most of the uncertainty of life. Plan it out and make good decisions, I thought, and life would hand me the desired results.

And so I planned, pinning my hopes on order and predictability. Life, for me, was an amusement park ride, and I was cruising along in one of those miniature antique cars, a stately Duesenberg or Model T or Pierce Arrow like they have at Six Flags—steady, no bumps or jumps.

But not anymore. Suddenly we're expecting twins, and I'm careening downhill in the Runaway Mine cars.

I'm fortunate that the mother of these children is more pragmatic than I am. For Karen, the initial shock has worn away quickly. She's set herself to reading all she can on the subject of twins and pondering the day-to-day implications of mothering two little ones at the same time. Here, a full six months prior to their arrival, she's already more mentally prepared for them than I ever will be.

From a breadwinner's perspective, there's just so much to think about: a second baby bed to buy, a bigger house, more life insurance, the inevitable minivan, two sets of braces, three kids in college at the same time, and weddings—all things that I wouldn't consider with such fear and trembling if we were merely anticipating a second child. But no; I'll soon have a litter to attend to.

There are also the social implications of the situation to contend with, not the least of which is the sheer, freakish novelty of it. Saturday, we went to Toys "R" Us to price double strollers. As we pulled one off the shelf, unfolded it, and began to look it over, I noticed other stroller-shopping couples, wide-eyed and curious, staring at us. They were buying the normal kind of stroller, of course, and whispering, rather indiscreetly I thought, about us. At that moment, I could empathize with every tattooed man or bearded lady who ever appeared in a carnival sideshow.

Then there are the ladies at church—mature, grandmotherly types mostly—who feign sympathy but, I believe, secretly find humor in our predicament. With a twinkle in their eyes, they'll approach me in the vestibule, take my trembling hand in theirs, and say simply, sweetly, "Bless . . . your . . . heart."

And everybody we know has a multiple-birth story for us—how so-and-so down the street didn't know she was carrying twins until right there in the delivery room, and at least we know ahead of time, or how cousin whoosis had two sets of twins, and can you just imagine? Either that, or they want to know if twins run in our families—wanting assurance, I suppose, that it's not something in the water, some exotic virus they could slip up and catch if they're not real careful where they sip.

Karen reminds me, "You're the one who wanted three kids. . . ."

"I know, I know. But this isn't what I had in mind. What in the world will we do?"

She has an answer. "We'll just love 'em and do what we have to do."

"Oh," she adds. "And we'll throw away that stupid plan of yours."

Waste-O-Matic

———— ◆ ————

THIS is the tale of a boy, a dog, and an imaginative homework project gone awry.

The boy is my seven-year-old nephew, Kyle, who is in the second grade. The dog is Sherman, an excitable Jack Russell terrier and house pet Kyle shares with his twin brother, Tyler. And the project . . . well, that's where I'll begin.

Kyle and Tyler came home from school a few days ago with an interesting homework assignment: find a household problem, create a device for solving it, field-test the device, and be prepared to demonstrate the solution to classmates at an idea fair a week hence.

Kyle knew immediately which issue he'd tackle. He bounded off the school bus, burst into his mom's kitchen, and announced that he aimed to rid the backyard of misplaced dog poop.

This is a significant problem in Kyle's estimation, for it's his job, along with Tyler's, to take Sherman the dog outside and clean up after him when the dog does his business in the backyard. The goal, according to Kyle, is to get Sherman out the basement door, across the grass, and to the edge of the woods at the back of the yard before he cuts loose. Unfortunately, that almost never happens.

Kyle asked his mom, "You know how when we take Sherman out, he can't wait and just goes in the middle of the yard and I have to clean it up? Well I've got an idea. . . ."

That idea turned out to be something Kyle calls the Waste-O-Matic. He arrived at the name only after his mother vetoed monikers like the Poop Cup and Poop-O-Matic, standing firm in her conviction that "poop" is not a word seven-year-old boys should be saying at school.

Kyle drafted his invention on a piece of notebook paper with the attention to detail of a seasoned mechanical engineer. He took measurements, listed supplies he'd need, sketched the device from various angles. Then he was off to the hardware store with his dad to gather parts. Drill a hole here, bolt it there, attach it up front, and eureka!

The Waste-O-Matic consisted of a stainless steel bowl, to which Kyle and his dad bolted a wheel housing, so the thing would roll. Then Kyle added bungee cords—two of 'em, of the same lengths, one end attached to either side of the bowl. The other end of the bungees would attach to Sherman's harness, of course, so that when the beast was taken outside, the rolling bowl would trail along behind him, ready to catch anything Sherman might, uh, drop.

With the contraption assembled, it was time for field trials. The young inventor and his dad took Sherman out to the driveway, put on his harness, and attached the Waste-O-Matic. "Go, Sherman," said Kyle, giving the dog a pat and a nudge. Sherman took a couple of hesitant steps and stopped, interested in the noises behind him—tiny wheels and the echo of aluminum on concrete.

"Go, boy," said Kyle, and again Sherman took a few steps, noticing this time that the noise only occurred when he moved. Hmm. Sherman turned his head, then attempted to turn around. There was that noise again. He barked and leapt forward, overturning the Waste-O-Matic. *Clang!* went the aluminum bowl on the concrete. Sherman yelped, startled by the noise, and before Kyle could grab him, bounded off down the driveway, the bowl clattering loudly on the pavement right behind him. *Ca-thunk, ca-thunk, ca-thunk . . .*

The little dog twisted and yelped as he ran, startled and confused by this strange, noisy thing that seemed to be chasing him. *Ca-thunk, ca-thunk, ca-thunk . . .* Out the driveway, down the sidewalk Sherman tore, through the neighborhood, until he was gone from sight, but not from earshot. In the distance: *ca-thunk, ca-thunk, ca-thunk . . .*

For a second, Kyle stood frozen, open-mouthed, on the driveway and watched the spectacle, then collapsed in laughter on the grass. Somewhere distant, Sherman was still on his tear—*ca-thunk, ca-thunk, ca-thunk.* Shortly, the din grew louder, approaching the house from the rear, and as Sherman hit the woods out back, the noise changed. Kyle heard the bowl bouncing off trees, stirring up birds and squirrels amid Sherman's panicked yelps. Then up the backside of the driveway the little dog rocketed, and into the garage—*ca-thunk, ca-thunk, ca-thunk*—'round and 'round until one of the bungees came loose and the bowl fell off. Sherman whimpered and hunkered down, exhausted, in a corner. The prototype Waste-O-Matic lay in dented ruins, its pieces strewn across the garage.

That next week, as Kyle debuted the remains of his ill-fated invention at school, it was attached to a lovely stuffed Saint Bernard. "My dad says Thomas Edison failed a bunch of times before he got a lightbulb," Kyle told his classmates. "I think the Waste-O-Matic just needs some fine-tuning."

PaPa's Turkeys

————— ◆ —————

THIS time of year, my thoughts turn to PaPa's wild turkeys.

One morning later this week, my PaPa'll slip out of bed just before sunup and pull on his insulated coveralls, brogans, and Crimson Tide ball cap. He'll grab his double-barreled 12-gauge off the rack in the guest room and step quietly down the basement steps, around the back of the house, through the aluminum cattle gate, and up the rutted tractor path that leads to the pasture. Bandit, PaPa's old pest of a dog, will bound over from the lawn chair where he sleeps and fall into step with PaPa.

At the top of the rise, as the sun's first rays color a crisp, clear November sky off in the east, PaPa may shiver. He'll squat there with Bandit, shifting slightly on the balls of his feet to ease the soreness in his hip, and he'll inhale the dewy aromas of mown hay and steamy cow dung and the coming winter. He'll squint, looking off down the hill.

And there, across the pasture, past the garden, in a clearing just beyond harvested corn rows on the edge of the woods, will be a flock of turkey hens. Twelve or fourteen of 'em, busily pecking and scratching the fallow ground for well-nourished slugs and forgotten corn kernels.

I suspect that Bandit, normally hyperactive and rambunctious, will know well enough to move carefully and quietly behind PaPa when PaPa stands with a soft grunt and starts down the hill, across terraced pasture rows to the garden fence, close enough for a shot. He'll get only two chances, each within a millisecond of the other—two barrels, two shells . . . maybe two turkeys. If his aim is true, feathers will fly, hens will squawk and scatter, and there'll be plenty of white meat for everyone in the family, right down to the eight great-grandbabies.

PaPa's been here before. Pick a year. From that very hill he's watched generations of turkeys until this late November ritual of his has become as instinctive as the hens' own jerky caution as they make their way amid the dry cornstalks. It's as natural as their soft gurgle and cluck as they forage for breakfast.

On that morning, a hallowed family tradition will continue, Lord willing. It's a tradition my family knows well— those of us old enough to gnaw a drumstick.

It wasn't long ago that I walked that path with PaPa, my head no higher than his waist, trying against my nature to imitate his easy movements and gentle silence and straining to catch a glimpse of our Thanksgiving dinner in the raw, off in the distance.

As if I were with him this time, this year, I can hear him instruct me on strategy.

"Now, Scotty," he says, "if we'll move real quiet-like down to the salt lick yonder and wait a spell, you may see th' ole gobbler hisself put in an appearance."

In my mind's eye, I watch for that gobbler and long for those easy days, seasons ago, when helping PaPa scout

Thanksgiving dinner was every grandchild's dream. This tradition, like going to Decoration Day in May or eating MaMa's fried apple pies or hiding Easter eggs in the pasture, is part of the glue that holds my family together. It makes us who we are.

Thanksgiving isn't Thanksgiving without the smoky aroma of one of PaPa's tender, wild birds wafting through the house; the gathering 'round of family and the asking of blessing; the heaping of plates and then biting carefully into succulent white meat, ever vigilant for buckshot, which can crack a tooth. There's the obligatory ribbing of my aunt Jenny as we recall the time years ago when she made a pecan pie for our gathering and forgot to put pecans in it. We'll talk a bit of politics and religion, then the men will gather in the den to watch the football game as the womenfolk clear the table and discuss their ailments.

It's this tradition, the very ritual of it, that reminds us of our blessings. The turkey seasoned with buckshot and MaMa's secret methods means that we're here together again, means that, despite troubles, we have much for which to be thankful. It also means that PaPa's still at it, taking care of his own. The color is fading in his eyes, and the morning chill seems sharper to him. But the turkey is on the table, right where it's s'posed to be.

This time of year, my thoughts turn to PaPa's wild turkeys, Aunt Jenny's pecanless pie, the sweet security and fellowship of loved ones, and the enduring worth of simple traditions.

At these moments I wonder if my Claire, almost two years old, will ever know this experience, this ritual. Who will carry this on?

Then, for an instant in my mind's eye, I see a man who looks suspiciously like me, but older, standing atop an Alabama hill in the chill of a November morning with a wide-eyed throng of grandchildren gathered 'round him as he points across a distant pasture at Thanksgiving dinner.

Winnie the Pooh
and Underwear, Too

———— ◆ ————

IT's not often I'm embarrassed by my underwear, but the other day, I was.

I had run to the gym on my lunch hour, hoping to catch a quick workout before some afternoon appointment. I grabbed a locker key from the attendant and dashed down the steps to the locker room to change from work clothes (a shirt and tie) to play clothes (gym shorts and a grubby T-shirt).

I went right to the assigned locker and, without a hint of modesty, commenced to do what I always did at that point in my gym routine: I started to undress.

Only after my trousers were down around my ankles did I notice my reflection in the large plate-glass mirror that ran along a section of the locker room. Only then did I recall, sheepishly, what I'd put on that morning.

In the center of that locker room full of Jockey-clad college kids, beefy weight lifters, and a few pudgy, puffing professional business types, there I stood . . . in my Winnie the Pooh boxer shorts.

I was an instant spectacle, hard to miss, or so I felt. Around the band at my waist, in large, inch-tall cursive letters, were stitched the unmistakable words: POOH AND FRIENDS, POOH

AND FRIENDS, POOH AND FRIENDS, and the colorfully embroidered characters that bedecked the scanty fabric on the upper part of my left thigh practically screamed, "This silly little man is wearing Winnie the Pooh underwear and is not to be taken seriously!"

For a long moment I felt vulnerable, juvenile, entirely unprofessional, as if I'd been caught sucking my thumb during a business luncheon or something. For an instant, I was traumatized by the statement I was certain my underwear was making about me.

I mean, Tabasco neckties are okay, I guess, if you're into that sort of thing, and a pair of Tweety Bird socks can be frivolous and fun on certain occasions. But what a man wears under his britches mirrors his soul.

At that moment my soul was bemoaning those shorts, a well-meaning Christmas gift from my two-year-old daughter, Claire. I can't blame her entirely, of course. I like them—they're quite comfortable, actually. And besides, it thrills Claire to no end when I wear them.

That's a story in itself. Claire's current fascination with anything Pooh-related includes these new undershorts, on which are pictured a pouncing Tigger perched on Pooh's chubby chest. Claire has developed the embarrassing habit of asking to see them, sometimes at rather awkward times: "Et me see yooa unna-way-uh, Daddy." "Daddy, show me Pooh unna-way-uh."

Now, society has come a long way since the days when Lucy and Ricky slept in separate beds and couldn't say the word "pregnant" on TV. But—I'm sorry—asking to see someone's underwear, especially your daddy's, still carries a social stigma, even in America. I pray Claire outgrows it before she's a teenager, or we're gonna have some real problems.

Those guys at the gym didn't even have to ask for a peek, of course. They got it, unsolicited and unintentionally, when I absentmindedly dropped my trousers—me, in all my whimsically domesticated glory—spindly legs, droopy dress socks, and all.

At that moment, my only consolation was the knowing wink and grin on the face of a grandfatherly-looking old gentleman across the way. That young man there, he was surely thinking, must be a Daddy. (At least, I hope that's what the wink meant.)

It wasn't much, but it was enough. I regained my composure, pulled on my gym shorts, and marched out to the free weights, ready to face the world again . . . in my Winnie the Pooh underwear.

Ada Jean

———— ◆ ————

I loved Ada Jean.

I loved her from the first time I saw her dip snuff, when I was five years old.

She would stand at the ironing board, taking a rest from the work shirts of my father's she was pressing. Beads of sweat would glisten on her forehead and upper lip as her big, fleshy fingers would twist the top of a small tin container that held the dark, strange-smelling powder. She'd pull open her bottom lip with her thumb and forefinger, lift the tin to the dark cavity of her mouth, and pour a modicum of the stuff into the waiting receptacle she'd created between her yellowed bottom teeth and lower lip. Then she'd return the top to the tin.

I was fascinated. No one else I knew dipped snuff.

Deposited in Ada Jean's lip, with saliva oozing into it, the snuff became a brown goo. With deadly aim, she discharged any excess liquid into an old cup. In her mouth, the dip made a lump in her lower lip, making her chin seem larger than it was. Her tongue wagged out over her bottom teeth and tucked down into the space between teeth and lip, to hold the deposit in place.

This distorted her speech. *S* sounds became *f*'s, and *r*'s became practically impossible, so that when she said "Listen here," it sounded more like "Liffen hee-yuh." It often was difficult for me to understand her when she spoke.

Ada Jean spoke quite a bit, but mostly to herself as she watched her stories on the TV. "Stories"—that's what she called the soap operas, and she was especially fond of *As the World Turns.* In the late 1960s, if it was noontime in Bessemer, Alabama, you could always bet that the television in our house would be tuned to WBMG, channel 42, where Ada Jean was transfixed by the lives of characters so different from herself or me or anyone else either of us knew.

"That Mif Lifa, she sho' do keep huhself in trouble," Ada Jean would say as the closing credits rolled, referring to the perils of her particular *As the World Turns* favorite, a character named Lisa—"Miss Lisa" to Ada Jean. Miss Lisa was rather irresponsible, it seemed to me, but then, I was only five years old. What did I know?

In retrospect, I'm surprised at how little I knew—or know now—about Ada Jean. She came to work for us shortly after my younger sister, Tammy, was born and my mother went back to her schoolteaching job. The turnip greens she cooked were to die for. She stayed with us for about five years.

Ada Jean was of inestimable age, the mother of two high-school-age girls, and she lived in what my father called—without malice, as far as I knew—"the colored section" over in Raimund Heights. She was a churchgoing woman. And she worked hard, sometimes too hard, like the time my father had to ask her to stop starching and ironing his boxer shorts because the starch chafed.

What I also knew—what was so apparent and what I remember still—was how she loved my parents and adored my sister and me. And that feeling was mutual.

I remember the first time I saw her. She stepped meekly into our kitchen, a black patent leather purse on her arm, knee-high panty hose rolled down around her ankles, her feet bulging in sensible shoes.

She wore cotton blouses and simple skirts, mostly—plain, slightly faded and worn. The skirts were secured around ample hips and plump thighs that I soon learned could convert into a spacious lap at the slightest urging from me. Ada Jean was fond of sitting down, and as fond of holding a child on her lap as my sister and I were of being perched there.

She smelled faintly of snuff and hair oil and perspiration. It was an exotic, lusty aroma to a child more accustomed to the light, airy scents of White Shoulders and hairspray that trailed after my mother. Ada Jean's was something darker, more exotic, unfamiliar to me, and not at all unpleasant.

Ada Jean neither looked nor acted like anyone else in my little world. For one thing, she was colored. That's what she called herself—a colored woman—even as her daughters were urging her to say she was black and to stop using what they viewed as another repressive, pejorative expression of a passing era.

I didn't think she was black at all. Her skin was the color of cinnamon, of rich, swirling sorghum, of fresh pecans, of warm Alabama topsoil. I was drawn to the deep, electric warmth of it, and I wished I were colored, too. Any old body could be white.

What's more, Ada Jean couldn't drive, or didn't. She certainly didn't own a car, and I've always assumed she'd never been taught to drive. So, early on weekday mornings, my father would leave home, retrieve Ada Jean from her tiny, ramshackle, clapboard house on Bullard Street and deposit her at our door before heading for work himself. It was a funny sight to see the two of them speeding down our street wedged inside Dad's little sardine tin of a Volkswagen Beetle.

To this day, I don't know how my parents afforded a maid. Although I wouldn't realize it until years later, we certainly weren't well-off. When my father's commissions from the insurance policies he sold were combined with my mother's salary, there couldn't have been much left in the till at the end of the month. But there was enough for Ada Jean—not just her wages and withholding taxes, which my mother dutifully paid, but also vegetables from the garden and daylily bulbs and hand-me-downs and all the other things that friends and neighbors give and take. Ada Jean was family.

I remember her laughing. Often. Heartily.

One afternoon, when my mother had made an appointment for my sister and me to have our portrait made at Olan Mills, Ada Jean was charged with getting us dressed for the occasion. Mother planned to hurry home after school, load us in the car, and off we'd go to Olan Mills, Ada Jean in tow.

Mother left Ada Jean instructions to have me dressed in a certain suit, with clip-on tie, and to put my two-year-old sister in such-and-such a dress. Dutifully, Ada Jean had us scrubbed and ready when Mother pulled into the driveway at three-thirty, and we all piled into the car. Ada Jean rode in the backseat to look after Tammy.

When we reached Olan Mills, Mother eased the car into a parking space until the front tire bumped against the concrete curb. She was opening her car door as Ada Jean loosened

Tammy from her seat, when Ada Jean let fly a whoop from the backseat. I was on my knees peeking over the seat in an instant.

"What, Ada Jean? What is it?" my mother asked, concerned.

"Lawd have mercy, Miz Brunner, dis baby don't have on no unduh-drawers!" Ada Jean shrieked, then convulsed into deep belly laughs that left her gasping for air. Not even my mother could keep a straight face in light of Ada Jean's apparent oversight. In my recollection, it's the only time a member of our family has ever had her portrait made without her underpants.

It wasn't long after that that Ada Jean left us. I was never sure why. Something about her daughters thinking she could do better.

Awhile back I saw Ada Jean again for the first time in more than twenty years. She came to my sister's wedding. Older, of course, a bit stooped, not quite as plump as she once was— she seemed careworn, but grinned broadly when she recognized me.

"It's so good to see my baby," she whispered. "It's so good to see my baby."

We embraced, and I was struck by how small she seemed, by how much had changed since those days when, as a small boy, I'd burrowed my face in her skirts to hug her goodbye at the door. So many of the times she'd bent over to kiss countless skinned knees and elbows, all the peanut butter sandwiches she'd made, the soap operas we'd watched together—they came back to me.

I allowed myself the momentary presumption that Ada Jean, perhaps, had encountered more than her share of difficulties since I'd seen her last, and I was reminded of a line from a Langston Hughes poem I'd read in college: "Life for me ain't been no crystal stair."

As she pulled away, a tear rolled down her cheek. Mine, too.

The Great
Sweet-Potato Pie Debate

———— ◆ ————

ALL the seasonal hall decking and chestnut roasting that Thanksgiving ushered in has fanned an ongoing debate at my house. At the very time of year when visions of sugarplums should be dancing in our heads, my wife and I, good Southerners that we are, find ourselves disagreeing (again) about food—specifically, that holiday delicacy of delicacies in the South, sweet-potato pie.

This is more than just an academic debate, for here in the South food is serious business. I mean, you just don't go runnin' down somebody's sweet-potato pie or banana puddin' or squash casserole if you're not prepared to justify your argument.

It's a Southern thing—talking about food, arguing about whether one variety is superior to another, whether the collard greens at the Farmers Market Restaurant in Jackson are tastier than those at T. Culp & Spoon in Tupelo. Down here, we debate barbecue, whether Texas- or Carolina-style is better; we fuss over the right amount of sugar to put in a gallon of iced tea (at our house, it's a cup and two thirds); and we even give prizes for the best sweet pickles and scuppernong jelly at the Neshoba County Fair every fall.

In the South, food is one of the few remaining polite topics for conversation. We've seen far too many fights break out when the discussion turns to politics or religion or football. But you criticize the preacher's wife's red velvet cake, and you'll start an intellectual discussion that could go on for hours. Folks down here can spend entire evenings recounting mouthwatering details of long-ago meals at Grandmama's, remembered with the same wistfulness and emotion that other folks reserve for more intimate matters. Who else but a good Southerner could find a plate of fried chicken and mashed potatoes sensual?

It's from that cultural predisposition toward food talk that our great sweet-potato pie debate sprang.

See, Karen and I both like sweet-potato pie. In fact, we *love* sweet-potato pie, so it's not a matter of pro-pie versus anti-pie. What we disagree on is the style of the pie, the substance of it, the taste. Although we grew up a mere ninety miles apart, both in the heart of the Deep South, our families' philosophies of sweet-potato pie are quite different. She likes it plain; I like it fancy.

In Karen's family, sweet-potato pie is an institution, a fixture at any family gathering, usually made by MawMaw Rhodes, and perfect for topping off a Sunday lunch of chicken pie, stewed okra and tomatoes, and butter peas. As best I can tell, the recipe is simple: sweet taters, eggs, sugar, evaporated milk, and just a skosh of vanilla. Bright orange in color, it's thoroughbred in every way.

And while it doesn't hold a candle to MawMaw's carrot cake, it's still good. Heck, it's very good, sorta like the way eating at the Cracker Barrel is very good when you've gone a week without home cooking. But it's not what I grew up on.

In my family, Mother's sweet-potato pie is more like . . . well, an extravaganza, full of variety and texture and best served after dinner on a pretty plate with a steaming cup of coffee. The recipe changes from pie to pie, and on any given occasion may include eggs, evaporated milk, vanilla, cinnamon, brown sugar, nutmeg, cloves, pecans, coconut, orange rind, and of course, sweet potatoes (for taste). Its surface is a wizened, noble bronze; it's a concerto of mouthwatering tastes, the alpha and omega of holiday desserts. But that's just my opinion.

Karen thinks my version is too much. "That's not a pie," she says. "It's a casserole."

"Call it what you will," I say. "I thought you liked sweet-potato casserole."

"I do," she continues. "But what's the point of having casserole and pie that taste just alike?"

She's got me there, so I decide to wow her with some philosophical gobbledygook. "Don't you think our taste in sweet-potato pie might be allegorical, an indicator of who we are?" I say. "Could it be that sweet-potato pie says something about our personalities?"

She doesn't fall for it. "You've been in too many psychology classes. Don't change the subject," she says.

I continue: "I like to think that my affinity for all that cinnamon and nutmeg and crumbly, butter-soaked brown sugar in my sweet taters mirrors my psyche, revealing a complicated, creative individual of eclectic interests; a guy who'd rather drown clinging to an interesting theory than float along on the security of a cold fact; a guy who wears bow ties and likes living on the edge on occasion."

She smirks. "Or maybe it just means you're a sucker for cinnamon."

"Well," I say. "Perhaps your affection for plain-Jane pie may reflect your judicious, commonsense, straight-shooting manner." I'm patronizing here, and she knows it.

"Or maybe I just like MawMaw's brand of pie best of all," she says.

Karen's right, of course. As these food arguments go, it's all a matter of personal taste. Because home cooking doesn't impinge on any deeply held moral or political conviction, it's one issue in the South that we can discuss ad nauseam, then agree to disagree without rancor.

And the fact is, when it comes to sweet-potato pie, you won't find me turning down either variety.

This holiday season, may all your desserts be worth arguing over.

4:00 A.M.

———— ◆ ————

AT 4:00 A.M. no one would mistake me for Father of the Year.

There in the dark, half awake, one of my infant sons thrashing and wailing in my arms, the other in my wife's, some part of me loathes babies—only in passing, only for the few minutes it takes for them to gulp down, then burp up, four or five ounces of foul-smelling formula—but sleepy as I am, I'm certain I loathe them.

I hunker down and mouth a prayer to the saint of speedy feedings.

Maybe at four A.M. I'm unfit to be a father. If I could just get some sleep. One night, uninterrupted. Eight little hours. That's all I ask.

Oh, please stop screaming in my ear. Please hush. Hush. Hush, little one! Please.

At four A.M. my life is out of my control, and I'm slave to my infant sons and their three-hour feeding schedules.

Maybe I doze off for two or three seconds, propped up against the headboard of the bed. The bottle drops from my fingers. Formula dribbles on the bedsheet. Jackson shrieks, and I control my desire to curse. Barely. *Here, son . . . take the bottle. Here ya go. Please take the bottle. Please. Please. There ya go. . . .*

The first time around, with our daughter, Claire, it was simple—for me at least. She was so easy to love, a joy to my waking hours, for she made no demands on my slumber. Dutifully, Mommy awoke to handle her twice-nightly feedings so that Dad could be fresh and rested for work the next day. But now, with twins . . . Mommy doesn't really give a rip whether Dad is fresh and rested or not.

We're done; need to burp. *Here we go, buddy. Burp. Burp, child. Please burp. I know you have a burp in there . . . Yow! Now that was a burp. Ooh . . . blech! . . . formula breath. Oh . . . don't. Don't cry. I didn't mean it. Please, hush. Hush. Please. . . . Daddy's so tired. . . .*

There is a difference between loving a baby and loving the *idea* of a baby—the concept of baby, of cuteness and innocence in its purest temporal form—but we seldom realize it until the former is bundled in our arms, and by then it's too late. We've been snookered. Four A.M. comes and we're jolted awake by cold reality: a ten-pound bundle consisting of a loud noise at one end, complete lack of responsibility at the other. Make that two bundles.

Sometimes it scares me what I think and feel there in the dark. Some mornings, rudely awakened in the wee hours by two infants who have every intention of beginning their day right then rather than going back to sleep, I feel like screaming, running out, stowing away on the next freighter north.

I've begun to question my self-control. There have been times during the past few weeks—usually at four A.M.—when I'd sooner sell my three-month-old boys to the circus than spend another moment dealing with them. Maybe I'm a monster, a sociopath. At four A.M., I realize I certainly don't have what it takes to be a mommy. I'm barely making it as a dad.

Okay, buddy, let's get you back in bed. Don't pout up. Please don't . . . hey, I'll rock you. How's that? Daddy and Jackson will rock. See, Mommy has Pate. . . . They're rocking. . . . Good boy. We'll rock, too.

If I despise them, even for an instant, it's in the same way that a child hates to come indoors at the close of a summer day, the way a man despises shaving for the umpteenth morning in a row. It is an immature, selfish, altogether superficial feeling that exists only for that moment—a cloudburst that comes in the night, then dissipates, dries up. It frightens me but causes no damage, and by sunrise there's no sign it has ever been.

They're just so helpless—infuriatingly, endearingly, frighteningly helpless—and somehow I manage to love them for it. Or through it. Love is the socially acceptable emotion here, of course. But at four A.M., this love is not exactly affection, not warm feeling—not yet, anyway. No, this is love, the verb—an action word, something you do because at four A.M., you simply have to. At this hour, with the child writhing and squalling in my sleepy arms, it's hard to muster more than love, the verb.

I think he's gone now. Maybe. The other one, in Mommy's arms, is out like a light, and she carries him gingerly to bed. Mommy is the lucky one tonight. *You asleep, buddy? Hmm? Good . . . good.*

They can fool you, ya know—feign sleep, then, when you struggle to your feet to carry them to the crib, erupt into uncontrollable squalls. *Ha, Dad! Gotcha!* But his eyes are closed, his breathing is slow and steady, and doggone it, he's wearing that beautiful, helpless, angelic little face . . . the one I manage to adore.

At that moment, around four in the morning, I'm glad these boys don't quite know me yet; glad they won't remember my immaturity, my selfishness; glad I have years ahead to work on becoming the kind of daddy they and their mother think I am.

About the Author

———— ◆ ————

Bessemer, Alabama, native R. Scott Brunner spent frequent childhood afternoons roaming the hills and hollows of his grandparents' farm near Parrish, Alabama, picking peas, fishing with his grandfather, and eating his grandmother's home cooking. Those experiences and others like them led to these essays, observations and reminiscences about life and relationships in the South. He earned a bachelor's degree in finance and English from the University of Montevallo and a master's degree in political science from Auburn University at Montgomery. He is an association executive in Jackson, Mississippi. Scott and his wife, Karen, have a three-year-old daughter, Claire, and twin one-year-old sons, Pate and Jackson. Scott is a commentator on NPR's *All Things Considered* and Public Radio in Mississippi (PRM).